Café Racer
the motorcycle

*Featherbeds, clip-ons, rear sets,
and the making of a ton-up boy*

Mike Seate

Café Racer
the motorcycle

*Featherbeds, clip-ons, rear sets,
and the making of a ton-up boy*

Mike Seate

Foreword by **Dave Degens,
Dresda Autos, London**

PARKER
HOUSE

Parker House Publishing Inc., 1826 Tower Drive, Stillwater, MN 55082, USA
www.parkerhousepublishing.com

ISBN-13: 978-0-9796891-9-2
ISBN-10: 0-9796891-9-8

Book design Mandy Iverson
Cover design Amy Van Ert-Anderson
Editor Kristal Leebrick

Manufactured in China

10 9 8 7 6 5 4 3 2

Contents

Foreword

By Dave Degens of Dresda Autos, London

I feel very lucky to have been able to spend my life and make my living doing what I love best; building and racing motorcycles.

It all started with an old Matchless 350cc. I was working doing a part-time job at the time with my father, helping him deliver film to cinemas in his van – we used to go round the North Circular and we'd stop off at the cafes on the way, places like the Ace, the Busy Bee and Johnson's, all places motorcyclists used to meet. I painted a couple of houses to get forty quid together to buy this ex-WD Matchless someone had hand painted black, and started going over to a cafe called the Queen of Hearts in Whitton High Street – it might still be there. I must have been about sixteen I suppose and the other riders there were all a bit older than me and had bigger bikes. The owner of the caff, John Carpenter, had a Vincent, a Black Prince I think it was. Ian Wallace had a 500cc Dommi, Johnny Fields a Velo 350cc and Frank Walters ran this 7R with a '54 Tiger 110 lump in it. Looking back, that's where I learnt a lot about riding quickly, because I really had to wring everything out of my bike just to keep up.

It's where I started to get interested in tuning, too. I put all the go-faster bits I could afford on my bike to try and stay in the running; a home-made ally nose-cone fairing, handlebars turned upside-down. I even took a great big 'dreadnought' file to the barrels and shaved off a load of metal to 'up' the compression. I just did it by hand, judging it by eye, and managed to get it within five thou on a vernier. I remember I raced over to Twickenham, splashed out on a trick high compression piston from Blays the grass-track specialist and got that old bike going up to about eighty. We used to race from Whitton to Twickenham along the Chertsey by-pass, we called it the 'By-Pass Stakes' – until the police got interested.

At the weekends we all used to go off on what came to be known as 'Mawkin's Mystery Tours' because Peter Mawkin on his big BSA 650cc with a sidecar always reckoned he had a route planned – but he never really knew where we'd end up, or how we'd get home. It was always good fun though. We used to meet up at the Queen of Hearts and then head off to places like Box Hill or down to the sea at Climping. There was a pub we used to go over at Effingham that served good old-fashioned scrumpy cider. One time I do remember we were all coming back across Salisbury Plain from somewhere when my efforts with the dreadnought together with the standard wide ratio gearbox resulted in a bent valve. One of our gang, Johnny Gray, gave me a tow home behind his bike using the belt off a waxed coat and a bunjie strap—one of the old wartime ones off a plane, they were a lot stronger in those days. Johnny's bike was the first Triton I ever saw. This must have been about 1955, and it was a '54 T110 in a '53 Manx, with the old lay-down Norton box. I think we got home faster than my bike went on its own!

I did my first race in 1959 at Thruxton on a stripped-down road (BSA) Goldie. I was going all right and was looking to take the lead in the Final until someone inside me fell and took me off. But I'd got the taste; the £12.00 I earned for winning my heat was good money compared to the four or five pounds a week I got working for my dad. In 1960 I bought a 7R off Geoff Monty on hire purchase for £400. I had a pretty good season – at the end of it he bought the bike back for £425 because it had got a good reputation. But just as I was getting going, I got hauled off to do my National Service.

Geoff agreed to sponsor me for the two years I was in the army and my CO was quite good and gave me time off for racing – as long as I won! With my prize money I bought a little scooter shop in Putney called Dresda when I was de-mobbed and I started selling and working on bikes. Then in 1965 I put together my own Triton and entered the Barcelona 24 Horas. Racing with Rex Butcher, we came in first against all the Italian and Spanish factory teams. That really established the Dresda Triton and got us on the map.

When we got back from Spain, John Ebbrel from the *Motor Cycle* borrowed the bike to run it from Land's End to John O'Groats – and it never missed a beat. Suddenly we had orders coming in from everywhere. I think it was the reliability that made it so popular. That coupled with seeing the bike win at hard scratching circuits like Brands Hatch on a Saturday. It really was a bike you could use to go to work on all week and win a race on at the weekend. A proper café racer.

I've done all sorts of different things over the years; just to rub it in I won again at Barcelona in 1970, this time with Ian Goddard, on a bike with a special frame I designed around the unit construction Triumph engine. Later I built frames for the Honda 750 four cylinder engine that won the Bol d'Or for Japauto and the development of those machines led me to design box-section swinging arms, twin headlamp fairings, four into one exhausts – I'm always experimenting. I can't count the different engines I've built special frames

for. Later this year we're sending a 1,200cc JAP in a Manx frame to the Bonneville Salt Flats to challenge the speed record.
But in the end, the café racer I always seem to come back to is the Triton.

Whatever your favourite café racer is, enjoy it.

Dave Degens

Introduction

As with nearly all motorcyclists, my emergence into the sport was deeply influenced by my surroundings. To natives of the hard-nosed industrial town of Pittsburgh, Pennsylvania, motorcycles meant Harley-Davidson, no question about it. In the center of the U.S. steel-making industry, riding an American-made motorcycle was the only way to go; merely firing up the engine and riding across town was perceived as an inherently patriotic act.

I never saw any other types of motorcycles because they simply weren't part of the local motorsports landscape. Members of the local police department's motor corps performed their duties on Harleys. In those days, as the U.S. steel industry was dying at the hands of foreign competition; riding a Honda to work at a mill or foundry meant risking slashed tires or worse.

Falling dutifully into line, I scrimped and saved from various teenage fast-food jobs and an uninspiring stint in the Army Reserves until I could enter a local Harley-Davidson dealership and exchange my savings for a 1969 XLCH Sportster. Done up in a very Age of Aquarius motif of copious chrome, orange metalflake lacquer, and forks long enough to make cornering an unhealthy affair, the Sportster, in my eyes, was about as wicked-cool as a motorcycle could be. It didn't much matter that the well-worn Sportster's 61-cubic-inch motor was barely capable of propelling the machine above the 90-mile-per-hour mark. To my youthful ego, it was far more important to own a bike that guaranteed I'd be noticed by young lovelies from the sidewalks than to ride a motorcycle that didn't require its engine-mounting bolts to be retightened after every second ride.

But like many motorcyclists riding around in a cultural fishbowl, I experienced an event that was, looking back, truly transforming. Riding alongside my buddy Rich, who rode a similarly overwrought and underpowered chopper, I remember feeling invincible, as if the whole world—including the cars eager to grant us wide berth in the passing lane—knew that we and our motorcycles were the final word in crazy, sexy, cool. And then, unexpectedly, from the far reaches of my peripheral vision, I spotted a flash of metal and felt the low rumble of a parallel twin engine.

In less time than it took to write this sentence, a pair of extremely low-slung, silver motorcycles charged forward just a few feet from our rattling, pinned-to-the-stops choppers. Though the ride took place some twenty-five years ago, I can distinctly remember the odd-looking foreign motorcycles as if they'd just passed me during my evening commute last week. Instead of sitting upright with their feet kicked yards ahead of them like a chopper rider, these riders were bent lewdly over the massive, silver gas tanks on their machines. Their hands clutched handlebars barely longer than throttle twist grips and their feet were tucked far to the rear, giving the impression the riders were passengers strapped to a ballistic missile.

While my partner and I struggled to maintain 85 miles per hour with our tall handlebars and power-sapping open exhausts, the pair of motorcyclists (I'd only come to understand them as café racers years later) simply dropped their transmissions down a cog, as smoothly as a pair of navy fighter jets makes a synchronized mid-air turn, and blatted off into the distance.

To Rich it was a moment of ultimate embarrassment; once to our destination, he demanded I never tell anyone about how easily we'd been passed. I had other plans. The incident left me spellbound, to say the least, and I couldn't tell other riders about it fast enough. What sort of weird motorcycles were Nortons and BMWs anyway? How could a person ride a bike with tiny, stubby handlebars with their feet jammed behind them and their arses straight up in the air like an infant anticipating a thermometer? And what, I wondered again and again, did it feel like to go that fast?

My intellectual curiosity was sparked, and though I realize it only in retrospect, that ride fostered what has become a lifelong quest to understand those two spectacularly fast, unbelievably handsome motorcycles that passed me ascending Pittsburgh's Greentree Hill a quarter century ago. It would be a few more years before I'd abandon my dedication to cruisers and choppers in favor of café racers and modern sportbikes, but along the way, I managed to learn more about the history, development, and culture of café racers than I could have imagined. I managed to root out café racers on two continents, meet some of the most dedicated and talented motorcycle riders and builders on the planet, and feel the intoxicating sensation of accelerating on a hand-built street racer. I'd learn the difference between mods and rockers, between a slimline and a wideline Featherbed frame, and come to know that fast is always far, far better than slow.

I'd find evidence of parallels between the café racer movement and the worldwide chopper phenomenon that followed it by a decade or so. As the chopper riders would find, their lifestyle and appearance was deemed a threat by mainstream society and the mere act of riding a customized motorcycle was considered an antisocial act. The exploits of a fringe element of both subcultures would generate a lion's share of sensationalist newspaper headlines, whether in the case of mods and rockers rioting on British vacation beaches in the early 1960s, or the drunken thuggery of American motorcycle gangs a few years later. Both subcultures managed to capture the imaginations of filmmakers though the chopper oeuvre was far better suited to drive-in fare than the café racer or rocker genre, which was the focus of only a couple of films even at its zenith.

In time, the café racer scene, as the chopper riders and builders would later learn, may have given pause to Mr. and Mrs. Average, but the enthusiasm and style were undeniably attractive (read: *profitable*). As a result, the mainstream motorcycling community, including the parts and accessories aftermarket and the manufacturers themselves, would mine their

The author. Café'd at last! Kim Love

efforts for gold. It's no coincidence that today's popular and very profitable retro café racers, the Ducati Sport Classics, Voxan Black Magics, and Triumph Thruxtons are selling to an audience who might have been gobsmacked by the sight of a Triton or Tribsa in their youth.

What's universally cool about all of this is the enthusiasm for speed, style, and exhilaration shared by café racers of all nationalities and ages. Hang with street racers in inner-city America and they'll remind you of rockers hanging out in London's Ace Café parking lot. They share an obsession with gear ratios, top-speeds, cornering characteristics, and other universal café racer concerns. Today, a whole new generation of café racer enthusiasts are embracing the timeless style of street-based speed bikes, creating modified motorcycles that combine the midcentury style of the Manx Norton era with the formidable technologies and over-the-top funk of the streetfighter movement. It's a wonderful thing to behold.

See you in the passing lane!

Mike Seate

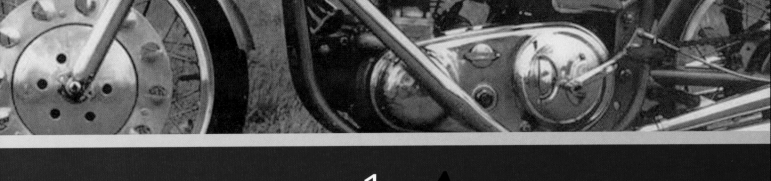

Speed Twin to Speed Triple

Like the four-minute mile before the record was broken

in 1954 by sprinter Roger Bannister, topping the 100-

mile-per-hour mark on a motorcycle was a tough nut to

crack. For starters, most motorcycles in the early half of the

twentieth century were designed not for outright speed but

for durability in all conditions. Though difficult to imagine

in our times of purpose-built superbikes scarcely capable

of ferrying home a loaf of bread and pack of smokes,

motorcycles designed solely for high-speed runs were the

stuff of either dreams or the very wealthy.

In Europe, as well as in the United States, most

motorcyclists in the 1940s and 1950s rode two-wheelers

for purely economic reasons: They were cheap to run

Page 10: *Award-winning British custom motorcycle builder Nick Gale and Mark Wilsmore of the Ace Café, London formed the Stonebridge Motorcycle Company in 2008 and promptly created "Little Miss Dynamite" as part of the 50th Anniversary Bike Build-Off sponsored by Wisconsin's S&S Cycle. The American aftermarket V-twin manufacturer donated the 1,600cc, 130 brake horsepower "X-Wedge" motor while Stonebridge created the dazzling, Manx lowboy design.*

two-wheelers for purely economic reasons: They were cheap to run and the same motorbike that propelled a rider to work was also used for off-road fishing or camping trips, hauling home a load of groceries, or taxiing the kids to school. Still, more than a few bikers were damned curious about the hidden performance capabilities of their otherwise dullish, multipurpose machines, and modifying motorcycles was an obsession from the sport's earliest days.

Britain has long been in the thrall of fast cars and motorbikes, with motor racing as much a part of the British sporting landscape as football or cricket. As early as 1908, W. E. Brough began producing motorcycles in Nottingham, with son George Brough opening his Brough Superior line in 1921. Billed as the

The 1956 BSA Gold Star Clubman edition, notable for its five-gallon alloy fuel tank, clip-ons and tall gearing, was one of the first, and most popular factory café racers. Author's collection

"Rolls-Royce of motorcycles," Brough's machines were amazing pieces of neo-Victorian elegance, featuring stainless steel, saddle-type gas tanks, exposed, overhead-valve engines, cantilevered rear fork suspension, and, for the landmark SS100 Alpine model of 1930, a top speed nearing 100 miles per hour.

One of Brough's most famous customers was T. E. Lawrence (of Arabia) the raconteur and military adventurer who needed a motorcycle capable of aircraft levels of speed in order to unwind. Lawrence owned several of these early superbikes and held a nation transfixed with his exploits until meeting his end after a motorcycle accident in 1935.

The prevailing wisdom holds that the precursor to the café racers of the 1960s were a breed of valiant, if not a little daft, British riders from the 1930s and 1940s known derisively as "Promenade Percys." Dressed in sheepskin-lined Royal Air Force flight jackets or army-surplus trench coats left over from World War I, this crew was notorious for making a lot of noise along the beachfront promenades at popular seaside resorts (where, coincidentally, the rockers would make themselves known a generation later). These early speed merchants formed perhaps the first recorded subculture of custom street bike tuners. The favored machines of the time were mostly small-displacement, British singles, including Velocette's KSS single, the venerable, oil-spewing Rudge Ulster, and the rigid-framed Triumph Tiger 70. These were affordable machines that were as much a challenge to keep running as it was to reach the then-incredible speed of 50 or 60 miles per hour on one of the few long, smoothly paved roads operating in Britain at the time.

As their heirs would in postwar Britain, the so-called Promenade Percys frequented whatever transport cafés would tolerate having a group of noisy, oil-weeping motorcycles on their car parks and dining rooms, habituating these places almost constantly. Though the press declined to sensationalize their exploits, the road-burners of the 1930s were every bit as fun-loving and reckless as the café racers would prove to be.

The "Percys" preferred to gather in groups and ride, at the highest speeds possible, from café to

A 500cc Goldie being put through its paces in its natural territory, a deserted backroad in the English countryside. Bauer Media

café, often with officers of the law in full pursuit. Individual cafés developed strong followings among local riders who formed impromptu teams and challenged each other to races whenever possible. Names such as the Orange Tree, the Tram, and Jack's Café faded faster than the smoke from a fried piston, but without the traditions of the pre-war riders, there may never have been a café racer scene at all. In time, their exploits—and, not to mention, their leisure time—would be eclipsed by World War II, but the die was therefore cast. Motorcyclists and roadside cafés became inextricably linked.

Though motorcycle racing resumed throughout the European continent and in places like the Isle of Man in the years immediately following World War II, motorcycling was, for a while, more a necessity than a passion for most. Those in need of cheap transportation included civil servants and returning war veterans, most of whom could not afford housing in those accommodation-scarce days, let alone a car. With most motorcycle manufacturers having turned their assembly lines over to the mass production of armaments between 1939 and 1945, what

The most pricey and the most desirable café racer of them all, the Vincent-powered special continues to be a favorite among the faithful. Patrick Godet

few motorcycles were available tended to be well-used workhorses five or ten years old. U.S. Army-issue Harley-Davidson service machines could be found, their stout V-twin engines and battle-tested running gear making them perfect for delivery vehicles and rural farm work. Development was slow in returning to the British motorcycle industry, but by the early 1950s, some of the seminal machines that would forge the heart of the café racer movement were already starting to emerge.

During the earliest days of the café racer movement, BSA's vibey, single-cylinder 500cc Gold Star Clubman was the motorcycle to have for fast riders. BSA first produced a motorcycle bearing that illustrious name way back in 1938, in honor of a 1937 race win by rider Wal Handler who lapped the Brooklands circuit at a staggering 107 miles per hour. When the bike received the coveted Gold Star racing award for its outstanding performance, the corporate suits at Birmingham Small Arms were sharp enough to capitalize on the name, bestowing it on a mediocre little, 89-mile-per-hour machine previously known as the M24 Empire Star.

It wasn't until 1954 that the BSA Gold Star began to appear in the form for which it would later become so famous. Sporting an all-aluminum engine on both the 350cc and 500cc versions, along with a then-revolutionary eccentric rocker-tappet adjustment, the Gold Star was 1950s performance personified. Owners marveled at the

Pride in craftsmanship is a hallmark of the café racer engineer, exemplified by the team from John Mossey Restorations who cooked up this tasty, T120 Triton in a Mossey Featherbed frame in 2003. John Mossey

slickness of the Goldie's close-ratio transmission, which would catapult the lightweight road-burner to speeds just above the 100-mile-per-hour mark—and this on a motorcycle fresh from the showroom floor.

By fiddling with different gearing or larger capacity Amal GP carburetors, some owners could cruise well past the 115-mile-per-hour mark when revving toward the Gold Star's liberal 8,000-rpm redline. It's worth noting that in today's market, where well-heeled riders can purchase $75,000 replicas of Ducati's Desmocedici V-4 Grand Prix racer, the concept of marketing replicas of track-ready machines is far from new. BSA's Gold Star Clubman was marketed on the heels of whatever race victories the factory could tally at Britain's road-racing circuits, and the various accessories filtering slowly from a nascent aftermarket—from

swept-back exhaust systems to high-compression piston kits—predated the Dynojet Power Commanders and big-bore titanium exhaust systems flogged at today's performance enthusiasts.

Of course, for all its svelte lines, beautiful chrome and alloy bodywork, and revvy nature, the Gold Star was far from a perfect motorcycle. Its throttle required vigorous twisting from a dead start in order to launch quickly, and that single piston could easily suffer from overzealous abuse, requiring new rings (and for racers, new clutch plates) at a sometimes debilitating rate.

George Brough's SS100 Superior satisfied the British nation's craving for two-wheeled acceleration during the pre-war era and created the template for hand-crafted, finely tuned streetbikes. Author's collection

The popularity of the big singles continued throughout the early café racer period with machines like the Matchless G45 and G50 making their mark in road-racing and the road-oriented Matchless G50 CSR and Vincent Comet taking the thumper battle to the streets. But that raw, rhythmic exhaust note was eclipsed in 1954 when Triumph introduced its remarkable T110 twin. Designed, as were nearly all motorcycles at the time, with a pre-unit construction (that is, with the engine and gearbox working as separate units connected by a primary drive) the T110 was nevertheless a great leap forward in the British bike community. Instantly faster from a dead start than the BSA Gold

Star, Matchless G50, or in the right hands, a Manx Norton, by the 1960s the Triumph had all the other British firms abandoning single-cylinder machines in favor of the parallel twin-engine layout.

The T110 was not the first success Triumph had enjoyed using a twin-cylinder layout. Back in 1939, designer Edward Turner made quite a splash in the two-wheeled community when he introduced the Speed Twin, a handsome, 26-horsepower, 498cc roadster. With its tiny drum brakes, tubular steel cradle chassis with rigid rear suspension (riders could seek solace in a saddle balanced on a pair of small, chromed springs), and a four-speed transmission, the Speed Twin accounted nicely for itself by reaching a top speed of 93 miles per hour. Turner's basic design, with its overhead valves and relatively smooth-running drivetrain, was so well executed and infinitely adaptable that it was copied by Norton during the 1940s. It would eventually form the basis for all of Triumph's machines until the factory's 1982 demise, with the exception of the three-cylinder Trident 750 (although this was in reality was really a three-cylinder twin).

Norton had earlier caught the twin-cylinder bug, despite the factory's engineers complaining that the engine layout caused too much vibration. Nevertheless, as the public clamored for twins,

Triumph's handsome, durable Bonneville was easily the most ubiquitous roadster of the café racer era and its 42-horsepower, parallel twin engine a sought-after powerplant for specials. Simon Green

Norton offered up the Dominator 7 back in 1948. The machine was something of a technological halfway point for Norton, who could boast of telescopic, "Roadholder" forks that were among the best in the industry. The rear end remained a fully rigid affair, however, until 1954. Norton's early experience with its iron-barreled, pushrod-operated, 500cc twin Dominator laid the groundwork for the future models, including the beloved 750 and 850cc Commandos of the 1970s.

Along the way, Triumph continued developing its popular twin-cylinder machines, addressing various problems with handling (frames weren't stout like the Norton Featherbed and tended to flex in high-speed corners) until getting the formula just about right with the introduction of the first unit construction T120 twins at the close of the 1950s. The new machines featured tubular cradle chassis vastly improved over previous models. The one-piece gearbox/engine/primary-drive powerplants saved power that had traditionally been lost between the separate engine units. Twin Amal carburetors could be a bother to synch, but when running properly, boosted power to 46 horses, which was good for 115 miles per hour—and that's before owners began tinkering with exhausts and other ancillaries.

By this time the Bonneville had been named in honor of the famous Salt Flats in Utah where, in 1956, Triumph rider Johnny Allen broke the land speed record. Allen may have been riding a highly modified version of Triumph's 650cc air-cooled, two-valve twin, the rider and mechanics enclosed in a sleek aluminum fuselage with a wheelbase 9½ feet long. Even so, Allen's run reached a velocity of 214 miles per hour, and the ensuing publicity proved more than enough to inextricably link the Triumph name with massive speeds.

Triumph, eager to capitalize on the entire street bike spectrum, also offered customers a Tiger 100SS, a scaled-down, 500cc parallel twin that served as a junior to the Bonneville's senior performance prowess. The Tiger, being more affordable and lighter in weight, did generate its own loyal ridership among café racers, many of whom relished the idea of passing bigger-bore

The product of years of racing development, the multiple leading shoe drum brake reach a zenith during the café racer era before being supplanted by more formidable disc units. Author's collection

twins on a motorcycle that was more nimble and easier to turn than a larger machine. The Tiger, like the Bonneville's predecessor the Thunderbird (ridden by Marlon Brando in Hollywood's *The Wild One*), suffered aesthetic styling that was not to everyone's liking. Everyone, that is, under the age of thirty-five who did not puff on a pipe while wearing a set of wool slippers and reading London's *Evening Standard*.

In a word, British motorcycles during this period were impossibly nerdy-looking, as OEM

manufacturers had little interest in appealing to the small fraction of youthful riders in need of visceral as well as visual excitement.

Instead, the motorcycles rolling out of Triumph's Meriden factory, for example, may have offered impressive performance, but they were a stately, subdued lot, adorned with overly full fenders and flat seats just perfect for carrying home a week's groceries. Advertisements at the time generally featured artists' depictions of motorcyclists who resembled happy, smiling vicars, pootling to some unknown destination, adorned in very uncool rubberized coats, Wellington boots, and helmets that looked like the headgear favored by school crossing guards. The motorcycles featured ugly, ornate bodywork, best exemplified

The Featherbed Frame–
The Chassis that Launched the Specials

There are those who believe that without the Featherbed frame, the café racer movement may have never taken flight. While that may be a strong, almost fanatical opinion, it's hard to overestimate the influence and effect the Featherbed chassis had on the British motorcycle industry when it was introduced in 1950.

The vaunted chassis sprung forth from the busy easel of Rex McCandless, an Irish-born engineer charged with extending the life of Norton's Manx racer, a thumping, vibey little 500cc rocket that was considered nearly obsolete amidst the post-World War II onslaught of British twins and howling, Italian-made fours. The chassis, with its distinctive twin-loop design not only managed to bestow the Manx Norton with the corner-hugging accuracy it needed to compete against larger, faster machines, it would continue to influence motorcycle frame design for the next thirty years.

McCandless didn't come by his legendary design by accident. The former aircraft designer had been determined for years to create a motorcycle chassis that included effective rear suspension (most bikes were rigid or equipped with questionable, rudimentary suspension) and a perimeter-style design that was wide enough

to envelop the engine and, therefore, keep weight forward, allowing for rapid acceleration out of corners. McCandless experimented with methods to reduce engine vibration at racing speeds and techniques that would prevent gas tanks from splitting due to excessive vibration. There was a box-shaped gusset supporting the motor at the very apex of the top rails, which helped keep the vibes down and the entire machine running true. After building such a chassis for an old Triumph Speed Twin nicknamed "Benial," McCandless perfected the Featherbed design, with its distinctive horizontal upper frame rails that bolted to the engine's head for added stability.

In its initial outing at the 1950 Isle of Man Tourist Trophy races, British champion Geoff Duke was among a trio of riders who claimed checkered flags aboard bikes running McCandless's revolutionary frame. When team member Howard Daniel was interviewed after the 220-mile race around the grueling Island circuit, he replied that he was as well rested as if he'd just spent the day in "a bed of feathers." Hence, a nickname was born for the incredibly rigid new frame.

It only took a few years for adventurous street riders to realize the advantages of McCandless's

by the dreaded "bathtub" fairing surround on the 1950s Thunderbird models.

Few machines capture this strange blend of the stodgy and the exhilarating like the Vincent V-Twins of the 1950s. Founded by Isle of Man TT race winner and motorcycle designer Howard Raymond Davies in 1928, the Vincent was known for unparalleled build quality, stately design, and eye-popping performance in equal measures. After outsourcing engines from JAP during most of

their early years, one of Davies' employees, the Australian-born engineer Phil Irving, completed work on his own overhead-valve, 500cc single in 1935. The single was impressive, capable of 90 miles per hour in the Vincent Meteor and, later, the Comet form. A year later, Irving experimented with a crankcase capable of rooting two Meteor cylinders at 47 degrees, creating a 998cc, 45-horsepower twin known, quite appropriately, as the Rapide. This led to the development of

design; increased demand meant the Featherbed chassis were stock fitment for Norton's Atlas model throughout the 1960s. The design benefited not only from ingenuity but from manufacturing advances that took place in the World War II years. Previously, motorcycle chassis had been built using a system of connected cast lugs attaching the various lengths of steel tubing. As it sounds, this was far from the strongest means of constructing a motorcycle frame. A new process known as SIF-bronze welding allowed the use of lighter grade steels in the construction of racing chassis and, later, in the production of arc-welded frames for road-going Featherbeds.

So broad was the Featherbed's distinctive, box-shaped engine "compartment," that unorthodox specials builders soon found the elbow grease and backstreet engineering savvy to force all sorts of engines into place. One of motorcycling's first and subsequently most enduring parts aftermarkets emerged to serve the specials market, providing aluminum engine mounting adapters known as "Converta plates" that permitted the application of Triumph triple, massive Vincent V-twin engines and anything else that roared and went fast in between the rails. The design remained virtually unchanged for most of the Featherbed's production run; during the 1950s, Norton produced the broader version known as the Wideline for its Dominator twins, while after 1960, the Atlas rolled upon what became known as the Slimline Featherbed frame, distinguishable by its curved rear frame supports as opposed to the straight-line configuration of its predecessor. Genuine Featherbed frames are thin on the ground today, but for café racer purists, nothing else will suffice.

perhaps the most famous British motorcycle ever: The vaunted, very pricey, Vincent Black Shadow, a revolutionary, 50-degree, 1,000cc V-twin that used the engine and gearbox as stressed members of the twin-shock chassis.

Billing itself as "The world's fastest production motorcycle," the 1949 Series C Black Shadow was the Suzuki Hayabusa of its day. This was a piece of consummate British engineering capable of a top speed of 120 miles per hour, a speed few sports cars—and, more important, no police vehicles—of the time could achieve. The Vincent's spindly, 7-inch twin front drum brakes were barely enough to slow it from a high-speed run, but that's not what mattered. The fastest motorcycle in the world was British and that was enough. Well, almost.

Most self-respecting café racers couldn't afford the Vincent's heady price tag, and just as many derived more pleasure in convincing themselves and their mates that any duffer who showed up at

Norton's 600cc Dominator 99, introduced in 1956, offered a 100 miles per hour top speed superlative handling thanks to its Wideline Featherbed frame, but its heavyweight steel fenders, gas tank, and mild state of tune made it a perfect target for the café treatment. Bauer Media

the local café on a Vincent would have a damned hard time leaving their Norton or Triumph in the dust. It also looked like something Dad would ride, were he interested in two-wheelers rather than playing the ponies, what with its plain black finish, stainless steel fenders, and upscale marketing campaign.

So there the mighty Vincent sat, admired and derided in equal measure. Eventually, however, motors from crashed Vincents, be it the Black Shadow or the Rapide, began showing up

at breaker's yards and eager café racers couldn't quite help themselves. Though it's unknown who first installed a Vincent engine into the tight confines of a Featherbed chassis, he deserves some sort of medal for what had to be some serious perseverance. The Vincent's engine attached to its maiden frame at several points with unique mounting lugs; in some instances Vincent specials builders came to tears after realizing their beloved alloy engines expanded so much during a ride that they just wouldn't fit inside a Featherbed frame. Further modifications involved the machining of custom engine-mounting plates and the mounting of rear subframes directly into the Vincent's crankcases.

It was a daunting challenge for even the most experienced and gifted specials builder, let alone an amateur operating on equal parts guesswork and

elbow grease. Experts saw the melding of the two as mere heresy, opining that the Vincent was light enough, fast enough, and timeless enough of design to not need alterations of any kind. Still the sight of a broad-shouldered Vincent motor squeezed into the confines of a Featherbed frame, and the wicked amount of sheer thrust it created, was well worth the broken knuckles and ruptured bank balances. It was yet another arena where the work of café racer specials builders would come to influence the motorcycle industry in later years.

The difficulties and triumphs (no pun intended) in adapting disparate engines into frames produced by other manufacturers paved the way for bespoke chassis designers like Harris and Spondon, who worked similar magic with ill-handling, but superbly powered Japanese four-cylinder superbikes in the 1970s. Inspired by the likes of Harris and Spondon, Italian firms like Bimota emerged a few years later, operating on the same basic principle of adapting a properly designed chassis and upgraded forks, wheels, and other ancillaries to deserving powerplants. Surely, technicians in race paddocks the world over had experimented with blending the parts from various manufacturers before, but it is doubtful the practice would

23

Though few would have believed it at the time, the arrival of multi-cylinder racers like this Honda would toll the death knell for the British motorcycle industry. Note how closely the lines of this 1966 factory racer mimic the home-brewed café racers of the era. Author's collection

have attained such credibility had it not been for the likes of the café racer generation.

I consider myself fortunate to have once spotted a Vincent-powered special parked up along the Brighton Promenade during a rocker reunion rally some years ago. After I knelt and crawled about the bike to study it from as many angles as possible, the owner approached, resplendent in pudding basin helmet, waxed cotton jacket, and a bristly white mustache. He cheerily explained the rather complex starting procedure, which required what appeared to be an elaborate ritual involving compression release levers, several priming strokes on the long, elegant kickstart lever, and probably a few muttered prayers. In a flash, the huge engine throbbed to life, the power pulses rocking the short-wheelbase motorcycle almost violently from side to side. With a flick of his boot heel, the owner pulled up the kickstand, struck the throttle twice, and roared off through a crowd of very impressed onlookers. Worth the trouble? Certainly.

But back in the 1950s, the Vincent wasn't considered so revered an icon among café racers, not just yet. It was, in fact, the yawning chasm between what a sub-section of the British motorcycling public expected from the machines and what the manufacturers were offering on showroom floors that would fuel the café racer movement immeasurably. Almost immediately, youthful owners of these staid expressions of British mechanical reserve began stripping off whatever parts they deemed unnecessary or impediments to outright speed. There was something of an unofficial competition at the time among café racers to see who could remove the most factory-installed equipment from their machines and still be road legal.

Typically, the first stock parts to be altered were the massive chromed steel silencers, which only encumbered a machine with unneeded weight while restricting performance. That a set of chromed, racing-style megaphone exhausts also sounded throaty enough to wake the neighbors (because your motorcycle was ridden after dark) was all part of the bargain. From weekend rider to club racer, street riders learned that faster terminal speeds could be achieved by ducking as low to the gas tank as possible. This was all but impossible on a machine with raised handlebars and bulbous round-top fuel cells, which precipitated street riders contacting the small-batch manufacturers of imitation Manx gas tanks for racing machines.

With a little clever backstreet engineering and a rubber strap, a large-capacity aluminum or fiberglass fuel tank could transform even the slowest street machine into a motorcycle that looked like a paddock refugee. There were other problems for performance-minded riders to surmount as well. The stock machine's rather tallish handlebars placed

Drawing on years of racing success, Britain's Velocette lured in customers with jaunty ads like this one from 1954: Wot? No helmet or leathers for the novice rider? Author's collection

a rider bolt upright into the onrushing air stream, causing all manner of problems. Not only was this seating position lousy from an aerodynamic standpoint, it looked nothing like the mad, dashing postures affected by roadracers, which is where most café racers drew their inspiration. Clubman handlebars had been available for years, offering a sensible compromise over full clip-ons, which limited steering lock and low-speed control, both of which were needed during street riding. But due to the exuberance of youth, clips-ons suddenly became quite the vogue. Not only was it fashionable to outfit your Norton or Ariel with a set of stubby, racing-style handlebars, certain café racer clubs took great pride in running their clip-ons as low on the forks as possible.

Classic café in the form of a Norton Dominator equipped with a rocker's dream full of aftermarket upgrades: in this form, the machine became known as the Domiracer and was a formidable street weapon. Note odd two-into-four exhausts and bacon slicer decorative brake detailing. Author's collection

A fully restored, if not over restored, Matchless G50 single; sold as a factory racer. Many of these impressive motorcycles saw street use where its 50 horsepower, 500cc motor rocketed it to a 135 miles per hour top speed. Author's collection

A perfect example of this can be seen in the film *The Leatherboys*, where a group of café racers exits the Ace Café forecourt, led by a BSA Gold Star pilot whose handlebars are so low they require him to lean out over the instrument cluster just to hold on. Credit was becoming available to working-class youths at roughly this time, and motorcycle dealers were eager to capitalize on weekly payment plans that kept their showrooms full of customers and empty of motorcycles.

Competition between brands for customer loyalty (and pounds) was fierce, which also helped fuel the café racer aftermarket. As early as 1951, Triumph offered its 500cc Tiger T100 in a "racing" version that would add high-

performance goodies, including racing cams, stronger valve springs, twin Amal Concentric carburetors as seen on the larger bikes, and even gear shifters that changed a transmission shift pattern into the weird, upside-down cadence of a true race bike. Never before had going fast been so easily attainable, and though café racers were considered an underground, grassroots subculture, there was collusion from the motorcycle industry even then.

With a veritable firestorm of performance possibilities emerging at this time, it was somehow inevitable that the classic hybrid special the Triton was born. Some reports find the mating of a Featherbed chassis and Triumph motor taking place as early as 1954, when British club racer Doug Clarke bolted a 650cc pre-unit Triumph 650cc engine into a frame that had been vacated by a detonated Norton Manx single. After a successful outing on the bike at the Silverstone circuit in Northamptonshire, Clarke reportedly attracted the eye of several Triumph factory representatives who gushed over the machine accordingly.

A few days later, however, the young racer was served with a cease-and-desist letter from the Meriden firm, suggesting he stop bastardizing their fine products with his own unorthodox ideas. Whether the folks at Triumph were aware of the circumstances, the cat was effectively out of the bag, and the Triton was soon as much a part of the café racer landscape as the '32 Ford Coupe, or Deuce Coupe, would be among American hot-rodders.

Part of the appeal of Tritons, above say the Tribsa specials and other hybrids, was the endless tuning capabilities. Triumph twins were among the most popular racing motors during the 1960s, with a plethora of go-fast accessories on the market. A rider with either cash or instant credit could up the power of a T120 engine with race-profiled cams, double-flow oil pumps, needle-roller bearings, and enough exotic exhaust tubing to give a pipe fitter

nightmares. Porting and polishing the four-valve heads could produce enough extra ponies to pip a pukka race bike off the starting line, while replacing a stock eight-stud, two-valve Triumph head with an aftermarket four-valve head from Weslake could offer an incredible (by late 1960s standards) rush of top-end speed and more midrange power that was sure to surprise your mates.

The Weslake head was a costly but effective modification that resulted from a partnership between aftermarket kings the Rickman Brothers and Weslake Engineering located in Rye, England. For their money, speed-starved café racers got a complete cylinder head featuring something called "pent-proof combustion chambers" along with barrel, pistons,

The existence of Triumph's own Thruxton factory café racer hasn't stopped clever builders from re-interpreting the new Bonneville to their own liking. Gas-charged shocks, sticky tires, and racing exhausts prove this one is built for speed. Author's collection

An emphasis on aerodynamics can be seen in the design of this 250cc Italian Parilla roadracer from the 1950s: the suede tank pad allows racers to lie prone and stay out of the windblast, while the "dustbin" fairing was rounded to offer the least possible wind resistant. Similar fairings would make a brief comeback on café racers. Author's collection

A rare café racer special in any age is this Norvin combining a Norton Featherbed frame and a Vincent 500cc Comet single-cylinder motor. Though most Norvins were built around the 998cc Rapide or Black Shadow motors, light weight and nimble handling makes this machine a winner. Bauer Media

and a set of eight "tournimonic valves." The kit bumped displacement from 649cc to 700cc and was so well engineered, the Weslake's valve angles were arranged at a high profile for maximum downdraft and fuel mixture while twin 32-millimeter Amal carbs atomized the gas. This was some real gee-whiz gear for young motorcyclists to call their own, and the resultant 65 horsepower churned out at the 6,500-rpm redline was pretty heady in a time when tuned twins were good for 45 to 50 horses, tops.

It has been said that if the minds controlling research and development at British motorcycle manufacturers were on-board for this kind of forward-thinking technology, the industry may not have collapsed with such completeness only a decade later. The box-shaped gas tanks, the rear-set footrests, and the humpbacked seats that formed the basic outline for any café racer has become so integral to sporting motorcycles that when the new Triumph Motorcycles Limited—reborn at the hands of real estate developer John Bloor in

1991—decided to issue its first retro machine in the 1994 Speed Triple, it shared a nearly identical silhouette with, if not the proportions of, a classic café racer. Long, low, and imbued with an undeniable sinister appeal, the Speed Triple came with a modern, four-valve, water-cooled three-cylinder engine, reliable electrics, and wide, grippy radial tires. But it was instantly declared a modern classic by the biking press, who, like consumers, had suffered through countless factory choppers when in reality, many riders wanted a modern, reliable version of the café racers of old.

The Speed Triple, like the Bonneville lookalike Triumph Thunderbird that followed, was accused by some of mining the company's past for styling cues, but both played their roles rather well. The initial Speed Triple was best when carving corners on a two-lane back road or showing off its muscular lines in town. The Thunderbird, which shared the 900cc Hinckley engine, was capable of multiple duties and, with its imitation garden-gate tank badges and mock Bonneville seat, looked good doing so. Not surprisingly, the success of these two models spurred a small but steady retro craze among motorcycle manufacturers in recent years, with Kawasaki releasing the excellent W650 and Triumph following up with a Thruxton café racer edition air-cooled Bonneville in 2005.

While these modern café racers are far quicker and more reliable than their predecessors, the rich history and romantic allure of pure, vintage Brit iron is still a force to contend with. I myself fell ill with a dose of the café racer bug, infected after seeing a Dresda Triton parked outside a London pub during

Sparsely trafficked roads, slow-police pursuit vehicles, and a dearth of speed cameras made British roads the perfect breeding ground for the café racer movement back in the day. Give 'er some stick! Patrick Godet

Bring on the Aftermarket

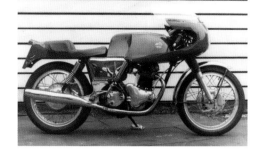

With today's burgeoning internet parts market and specialist magazines providing links to myriad parts and services suppliers, it's difficult to imagine life for café racer enthusiasts half a century ago. Britain in the 1950s may have enjoyed a heretofore unheard of level of economic prosperity, but the motorcycle aftermarket was largely the domain of serious racers or geared to serve touring motorcyclists who preferred Perspex windscreens and weatherproof Barbour jackets, not the go-fast accessories of the café racer set.

"No problem," answered back a youthful generation of enthusiasts who were eager to customize their street bikes for as much performance as possible. Like American hot-rodders, many early café racers simply sawed off the ends of their exhaust pipes and removed any extraneous parts in an effort to lighten their machines. That done, the full, chromed steel fenders that were universal equipment for British motorcycles were either cut short or removed entirely, replaced with smaller, aluminum models borrowed from on- or off-road competition machines.

Just as today, many street riders then were racing fans, and the design of the café racer closely followed the technologies being perfected at British roadracing circuits from Brands Hatch to the Isle of Man. Motorcycle manufacturers, always on the lookout for a street subculture to capitalize on, began serving up special Clubman editions of ordinary street machines, equipping the former all-purpose motorcycles with racy clip-ons or Clubman handlebars, smaller race-inspired seats, and swept-back exhausts mimicking those seen on short circuits.

By the early 1960s, a speed-crazed Britain and, subsequently, Europe, had sprouted countless small manufacturers and at-home builders eager to supply a generation of riders with the performance and style they craved. From backyard workshops came high-level, free-flowing exhaust systems guaranteed to win the admiration of your café racing peers and the unwanted attentions of the local police constables. Tiny, uncomfortable bum-stop seats done up in everything from mock-suede to faux leopard skin became almost fashionable for a time, while a few riders challenged aesthetics entirely by adding broad, "dustbin" fairings as

A Dunstall Norton Commando given the aftermarket king's full attention: Dunstall offered café racers everything from overbore cylinders to racing cams and high-compression pistons to then-exotic fiberglass fairings and gas tanks.

seen on exotic roadracers of the time. Their effect on a street-ridden motorcycle's aerodynamics was questionable at best, but even today there's an undeniable élan and mid-century cool to these road-going fiberglass shrouds.

Notable among the bevy of tuners that emerged during the 1960s was Paul Dunstall, an Eltham, south-London-based tuner and racing enthusiast who struck gold in the emerging café racer aftermarket. A meticulous tinkerer with racetrack successes to back up his formulas, one of his specially prepared Norton Dominators set a speed record at Italy's Monza circuit in 1967. Dunstall was known for disassembling engines and methodically grinding, polishing, and modifying intricate valvetrain components to make them lighter and, subsequently, rev faster and harder.

Though the must-have items for any ton-up boy was a fiberglass, Manx-replica Dunstall gas tank with alloy Monza, quick-action flip-up gas cap, rear-set footrests, and a set of stubby clip-on handlebars that were to be mounted as close to the front wheel spindle as possible, Dunstall was a tuning purist who didn't exactly ignore the need for ever-faster powerplants. If a rider could afford the terms, Dunstall would lighten his wallet for the price of bigger bore Amal carburetors, high-compression piston kits, polished and ported engine heads, double-speed higher-capacity oil pumps, and custom-ground camshafts. For the truly well heeled, complete café racers made-to-order or full Dunstall conversion kits that would transform an ordinary 650SS Norton into a stunning, and quite fast, Manx replica were readily available.

Dunstall, in his infinite wisdom, shared his leading suggestions for building specials with *Classic Bike* magazine a few years back, and the advice still rings with relevance.

Early speed still in effect exemplified by the 1936 Vincent-HRD Series A Rapide stopped at an Ace Café meet some 70 years after it was built. A ton-ten capability means this motorcycle can run with modern machinery. Simon Green

a vacation to the British capital in the early 1990s. I'd read about the stunning, purpose-built café racers in books for years, but in the United States they tend to be more rare than hen's teeth, so to speak.

My first Triton remains an important sighting in my life, though it caused much consternation for my poor wife, who had to delay a trip to the bookstores on Charing Cross Road for a half hour while I snapped endless photos of the motorcycle. Smitten, I returned home determined to recreate the motorcycle I'd fallen in love with overseas, despite most American motorcyclists—including many Triumph dealers and mechanics—having no clue as to what a Triton is. On a return trip to the U.K., I managed to track down a tiny shop on London's Chalk Farm Road where I purchased a rough-condition Slimline Featherbed frame, Later, I'd find my way to Unity Equipe, a specials parts supplier that emptied my wallet to the tune of a set of chromed, swept-back silencers, a beautiful Manx-replica alloy gas tank, and a tiny, bum-stop

seat barely large enough for my American-sized proportions.

Back home, my work was cut out for me as I'd been hiding an old stretch chopper powered by a unit Triumph Bonneville engine in a corner of our garage. Transforming this strange amalgam of parts into an actual, functioning motorcycle was an experience that proved both frustrating, inspiring, and challenging in equal measure. But with the help of Steve Collins, a lovably cantankerous vintage Triumph mechanic, the Triton eventually became a reality. After years of poring over Brit bike magazines extolling the handling prowess of Tritons, it was a revelation to find that they were not, in fact, exaggerating. As the owner of several modern sport

A Triton, the quintessential café racer, parked up at the Brighton Pier, a popular seaside retreat for the "Promenade Percy" crowd of the 1920s, and the rockers who followed during the fifties and sixties. Simon Green

The 500cc Velocette Venom's elegant, almost Victorian styling may have appealed more to a rocker's dad than to his buddies, but the Birmingham firm's singles proved fast, capable street machines. Simon Green

bikes, I was pleased to find the Triton capable of cornering with confidence.

In time, I entered the Triton in several custom and antique motorcycle shows. To be honest, aside from the frequent maintenance, the most harrowing parts of owning a Titan is explaining to my fellow

Americans just what a café racer is. Unfortunately, I'm not blessed with mechanical aptitude and the high maintenance costs of running a vintage café racer proved too much. We parted ways after an incident that illustrated just how much work must have gone into owning and riding a special back in the day: After the unwise decision to test the Triton's power on a dyno, the machine sputtered and blew out a gust of oily blue smoke before clanging to a halt in the middle of a busy freeway. I'd holed a piston during the dyno run, and without the funds for a full engine rebuild, the Triton I'd spent years building had to be sold.

When I related this story to a group of café racer enthusiasts at the Isle of Man a few years later, they just shrugged. "Why not just pull the piston, replace it, and be on your way," they suggested nonchalantly. Ah, if only. I then realized what a hearty and practical bunch the café racers must have been. They rode, after all, motorcycles bred without modern conveniences like electronic rev limiters, which meant an overzealous throttle hand could blow up a café racer like a 500cc grenade. Learning to repair and tune a bike back then was not only a necessity; it was part of the whole experience for most cash-strapped rockers.

Ours is a far more service-oriented society where broken motorcycles are towed to

Getting by with a little help from his friends: This café racer sidecar rig is equally at home on the street or short circuit though its spare, racing electrical system means seldom going anywhere without a few friends to offer a bump-start. Simon Green

With a lifespan that ran from 1931 to 1958, Ariel's Square Four was an odd powerplant designed by Triumph Bonneville creator Edward Turner. In essence a pair of parallel twin engines sharing a common crankcase, the machine became known as the Noriel in café racer form. Author's collection

Paul Dunstall's Top Ten Tips for Café Racers:

1. Don't waste time polishing the exhaust port. A port with a thin coating of carbon is more efficient than a polished item. Do polish the inlet port after reshaping to speed gas flow.

2. Lighten rockers with a grindstone, then polish with an emery board. Remove most metal from arm ends or parts that move the most.

3. Aim for a 70 percent balance factor for 650cc engines. Use copper asbestos head gaskets on spigoted barrels and reinforced fiber on nonspigoted types.

4. Larger, 1 1/2-inch Norton Commando exhaust valves will improve performance when fitted to 650cc Norton engines. Use bronze valve guides.

5. Only lighten tappets if a standard camshaft is retained. Leave tappets if a racing camshaft is used.

6. On racing motorcycles, main shaft bearings should be pegged to stop them from moving in their crankcases.

7. Use SAE 40-weight oil for road bikes and change it every 2,500 miles.

8. Use 1 1/2-inch spacers between the cylinder head and carburetor on road bikes. For racing machines, use 3-inch flexible induction piping.

9. Long bellmouths do not add performance when using Concentric carbs.

10. Separate exhausts joined by a balance pipe close to the cylinder head is the best layout for a road bike.

high-tech repair shops where factory-trained experts fix them. As a result, I never mastered the art of emergency engine teardowns and roadside piston replacement, so my Triton was, regretfully, sold off. Nevertheless, owning and building a special proved one of my most rewarding motorcycling experiences to date and, despite the difficulties, one well worth repeating someday.

As I'd discovered, style and creativity has always been as much a part of café racers as outright speed. Back in the 1960s, to address the dull black leather saddles supplied by OEMs, many café racers, imbued with the wackiness of London's emergent pop culture, fashioned faux leopard or zebra skin seat covers for their bikes, adorning their riding gear with similar accoutrements. In the drab, dreary streets of many a small village or industrial town, this must have been quite a sight, with a pack of ten or twenty similarly adorned motorcycles roaring by in a rush of noise and black leather.

In most cities and small towns, there was, by the late 1950s, emerging a coterie of motorcycle enthusiasts who eagerly distinguished themselves from the biking mainstream. They didn't care much for posted speed limits, and being hard-working types, they tended to travel at night, as evening riding was about all that their schedules would allow. It didn't hurt that Great Britain was just then tasting its first sample of a high-octane brand of popular music imported from the States, a sexy, hard-driving thing called rock-and-roll.

Over the years, sociologists have linked rock-and-roll with café racers through the jukeboxes that occupied a hallowed corner in just about every transport café. True enough, it would be several years after original American rock-and-roll acts such as Eddie Cochran, Gene Vincent, and Bill Haley and his Comets toured the U.K. that BBC radio accepted these bizarre new sounds. Therefore, it is quite likely that the first exposure to fast, driving music for fast-riding British motorcyclists came through the fuzzed-out speakers of an old coin-operated Seeburg jukebox.

Modern Bonneville given a full café treatment by Mark Selman of Michigan's BellaCorse, replete with alloy tank, raised pipes and Dunstall-pattern half-fairing. A one-make race series for the Thruxton held in 2006 has quickly brought the tuning aftermarket for this mild performer up to speed. Mark Selman

The author's Triton taking form, circa 1996; Slimline Featherbed chassis was found at a swap meet while the 5-gallon Manx tank and bum-stop seat were Unity Equipe items. Kim Love

Rock-and-roll provided the perfect backbeat for motorcycling, a sport that had its own, distinctive rhythms in the sound of a hard-revving engine and a whining gearbox. Many rockers, as they would soon come to be known, were elated to find that their American music heroes, among them Elvis Presley, also rode motorbikes and preferred to dress in black leather and even grease their hair and pile it high just like the Royal Air Force, often shortened simply to "raff," pilots the café racers idolized. It was all about speed, it was all about style, and it was about to become one of the longest-lasting pop culture movements ever.

2

Café Style: Black Leather to Brylcreem

Say the word *rocker* to most motorcyclists and it
conjures up images of those little machined arms
that operate the valves on four-stroke engines. For a
motorcycling subculture with a half-century of heritage
under its belt, the café racer cult remains cloaked in
obscurity in many quarters. At motorcycle rallies and
antique bike meets held in the United States, café
racer motorcycles are not unknown, but the style of
dress and the unmistakable competitive attitude seems
woefully absent from the equation.

I can't recall precisely when I first spotted a café
racer ridden by a motorcyclist dressed in the distinct,
form-fitting black leather and pudding basin helmet

of the rocker era, but I remember it leaving a powerful, lasting impression. That first exposure to rockers likely came from a few seconds of old, black-and-white newsreel footage of London during the 1960s broadcast on cable TV's History Channel. Or maybe it was in a photo on one of the retro-rockabilly albums I'd listened to while working as a music reviewer in the 1980s.

Unlike the intentionally messy, grease-stained denims of the hardcore Harley crowd, a look that some performance biker labeled "rolling haystacks" for their bushy beards and generally unkempt appearance, the café racers had a certain swashbuckling élan to their dress. Despite the fact that a motorcycle will push a more compact aerodynamic hole through the air without ape-hanger handlebars, chain wallets, and other riding accessories flapping in the breeze, most stateside riders, even those who preferred lightweight British bikes over Harleys during *The Wild One* era of the 1950s, still dressed more like the Western cowboys of lore than like the original café racers.

Look at photos of dirt-track racers competing in the United States and, until the late 1960s, most riders can be seen whipping themselves around the oval circuits wearing lace-up work boots, the ubiquitous blue jeans, and police-style leather jackets. Replace the half-helmets with a Stetson, and they could easily be transposed into a Frederick Remington painting. Western equestrian traditions also took precedence when early U.S. motorcycle designers created their ergonomic templates for street bikes.

Early Harley-Davidsons, Crockers, Hendersons, and Indians all reached showroom floors sporting buckhorn handlebars, their distinctive high-ride bends created to emulate the horns of longhorn steers from Texas. Still standard equipment on most Harleys and cruisers, buckhorn handlebars also provided motorcyclists with a sit-up-and-beg riding position that placed the operator's feet well forward and directly into the oncoming windblast. Built for traversing the U.S. continent's relatively long, straight highways in comfort, the cruiser riding style and its similarly cowboy-inspired dress was about as far removed from the café racer as motorcycling could get.

Why? Speaking to some who've studied the café racer cult closely, several factors coalesced to create the uniquely styled motorbikes and the equally distinctive look of the café racers. I once interviewed Maria Barry, a British expatriate living in the United States, where she operated Barry's Bike Badges, a small rocker clothing emporium. Barry, who had ridden a Triumph Bonneville in Britain during the late 1960s, recalls an age when most of her fellow motorcyclists followed professional roadracing closely, mimicking not only their machines but the gear they wore while riding them.

Modern rocker Matt Davis wears his café racer credentials on his arms, literally the British expat rides a late-model Royal Enfield Bullet and is dedicated to preserving the ton-up style. Author's collection

Restored café racer complete with rare, 1950s dustbin fairing adorned with skull and crossbones prepares to exit a café forecourt in London. Such fairings were eventually banned from roadracing but found a home on streetbikes. Author's collection

Full, one-piece racing leathers as worn by the likes of Hailwood and John Surtees were prohibitively expensive and mostly of the bespoke variety in those days, which meant they were thin on the ground for street riders. Leather was the chosen garment, whatever the number of individual pieces. And that the motorcycling establishment frowned on riders turning up on public roads or at work or in public houses dressed like a paddock refugee only made the wearing of black leather more of a rebellious act. Mainstream (read: old enough to be your dad) motorcyclists were content to cheat the

Vestments and black leather made for an unusual fashion statement but were common sights during the ton-up era as community-minded vicars embraced the rocker movement. Author's collection

Grand Prix stars like Phil Read, Mike Hailwood, and Geoff Duke were considered heroes and fashion icons. Because motorcycle roadracing had never developed much of a mainstream following in America as it had in the U.K., it is nearly impossible to gauge how striking an effect the sight of a Geoff Duke was to an impressionable young biker, as Duke roared down the front straightaway at the Goodwood circuit on his thumping Manx Norton. The British and European press covered motorcycle racing then, as now, as extensively as the U.S. media covers the World Series or Super Bowl, and it was not uncommon for riders to cover the walls of their garden sheds and bedrooms with photos of their racetrack heroes culled from newspapers and magazines.

The gear to have was, naturally, a black leather jacket similar to the styles worn by the racers, and, if funds permitted, a matching set of leather trousers.

Japanese rocker is a study in classic cool as he poses outside London's Ace Café: Original ton-up gear fetches a handsome price among Asian aficionados eager for authenticity.
Author's collection

notoriously damp, cold English air with stately, waxed-cotton overcoats from Belstaff or Barbour, though the ankle-length, black PVC or Thornide (read: a fancy way of saying *rubber*) "365" coat, thus named for its alleged year-round protective capabilities, was a popular choice. Many opted for a pair of Wellington rubber boots to keep their lower extremities dry during a ride, while helmets for the motorbiking mainstream tended to be white or off-white. These were typified by the Aviakit cork model, with its rather silly-looking bill, which one can only imagine was meant to ward off the sun's rays, hardly needed in midcentury Britain!

Any self-respecting café racer would have rather taken a bus than ride around looking like a two-wheeled postman, selecting instead one of Lewis Leathers' handsome Thunderbolt black leather jackets, advertised with "distinctive American styling," which, to any rocker in the know, was a veiled reference to the jacket worn by Marlon Brando in *The Wild One*. At just more than 9 pounds

sterling, it was not cheap, but even a Thunderbolt jacket had to be topped off with other must-have café racer gear like a set of Lewis's own Hi-Flite sheepskin-lined motorcycle boots (6 pounds and change) and Cromwell or Kangol "Jet" three-quarter helmet. It should be noted that jeans were eagerly embraced by greasers and youths in general when introduced to the British market, but that wasn't until 1951. By 1955, they were more widespread, as were leather jackets, both of which were considered hip and very American, and proved durable even in the worst conditions. It is worth mentioning the almost mythic appeal Brando's leather-clad "Wild One" had on teens during these years. Rock-and-roll had made quite a splash in England when acts like Chuck Berry and Billy Haley and his Comets first appeared in concert in the mid-1950s, and American rock music and a few R&B hits had been installed in thousands of café and pub jukeboxes to feed the fire.

The Wild One, in which producer Stanley Kramer re-told "Cyclist's Raid," a 1947 feature from the *Saturday Evening Post*, was about a riot staged by a gang of drunken California bikers. The film proved to be pure cinematic validation for a generation of early rockers and teddy boys, but in reality, few if any of the Brits saw the film. Rock-and-roll, with its sexual metaphors, raucous beat, and ability to cause riots, as Haley's film *Rock Around the Clock* did when screened in several European cities, had made some serious enemies, many of whom were MPs and other self-anointed guardians of public decency. As a result, *The Wild One*, which was nearly banned by church groups and parent associations in Miami, Cleveland, and several other U.S. locations, was banned outright from being screened in British movie houses.

Nevertheless, determined fans managed to secure a few copies of the melodramatic-but-enjoyable film, which was screened in youth center basements and, on occasion, at well-attended meetings of the vaunted 59 Club by projectionist and avid biker Terry "Tex" Childs. Despite the movie being successfully kept out of U.K. theaters, word of underground screenings spread faster than a rumor of free rock-and-roll records. As a result, Childs said, the huge crowds that showed up for the film made him wonder whether the authorities could truly have been unaware of the screenings.

Brando's inflated threat aside, there was little to be done to quell the flow of rock-and-roll into England. The music was everything the establishment hated and, naturally, that the ton-up boys loved. It was the music of disenfranchised urban blacks, poor Southern whites, and of teenage angst and alienation; there was the added attraction of more sex appeal in a four-minute Jerry Lee Lewis song than most British teens had experienced in a lifetime. The rapid rhythms were the perfect accompaniment to fast motorcycling, and it didn't hurt that the King of all American rockers, Elvis Presley, was pictured riding a motorcycle of his own.

In time, American rockabilly acts like Gene Vincent and Eddie Cochran followed Bill Haley for what turned out to be rather prophetic tours. Vincent, who often displayed on stage his own scars from a motorcycle accident, was an instant hit with the ton-up crowd, who dug his black leather stage gear and mile-high pompadour. Cochran was

California's revisionist rocker scene is kept alive by enthusiasts like Steve "Carpy" Carpenter who has developed a thriving custom motorcycle empire building CB750 Honda café racers.
Motorcycle Classics

Black leather, tea, and chips remain the staple of the café racer scene. Tall, white-topped boots are a look borrowed from RAF pilots during the Battle of Britain. Simon Green

Timeless cool: a Norton Domiracer and a black leather jacket. Simon Green

on in the U.K., frequently touring and performing before his legion of like-minded fans until his passing in 1971.

Visiting rocker hangouts in the U.K. today, it's amazing what a hold these early rockers still have on the collective imaginations of motorcycle riders. Elaborately decorated leather jackets can still be seen in profusion at café racer gatherings, the names of beloved idols like Eddie Cochran, Jerry Lee Lewis, and Gene Vincent spelled out in a thousand chrome studs. Expertly rendered paintings of these and other singers are also frequently displayed on clothing, and portraits of fabled early rockers in tattoos are more prevalent in recent years than could have been imagined half a century ago.

more of a traditional, pretty-boy rock singer, his songs offering an upbeat, radio-friendly contrast to Vincent's hiccup-laden, sex-tinged utterings. Both performers were virtually followed from venue to venue by crowds of café racers during their 1960 tour, which, due to a fatal car crash in Bristol, proved to be Cochran's last. Vincent, seeing how his work had inspired countless British rockers from Cliff Richard to Billy Fury, decided to stay

Perhaps this phenomenon can be attributed to the unique confluence of several sociological factors that struck postwar Britain at nearly the same time: A burgeoning manufacturing sector meant two-wheeled transportation was affordable and readily available; the re-arrival of coffee in Britain (after years of war-induced rationing) at roughly this same time meant kids were flocking to newly opened coffee bars and cafés just as the self-expression and "do your own thing" ethos of the beat and rocker movements took hold. As the Cold War escalated and the atomic age played its ominous hand during the 1950s, kicks were more important than ever. Having fun seemed to be the thought of the day, as we could all be vaporized in a mushroom cloud tomorrow.

However irreverent and rebellious toward authority the beat generation coffee-bar scene was, in its approach to life some say, the origins

Until Britain passed its helmet law in the middle 1960s, many ton-up boys rode bare-headed. Eventually, the Everoak helmet became a beloved fashion icon. Simon Green

Café racer etiquette demands riders to enter and exit a transport café forecourt at as brisk a speed as possible—watch out for greasy chip wrapping on the way in! Simon Green

During the café racer era, few riders could afford this level of adornment—a burgeoning rocker clothing market means today's leatherboys can flash some serious style. Simon Green

Members of the 59 Club prepare for a burn-up, circa 1963; note the mix of weatherproof Barbour jackets and leather riding gear. Author's collection

of the ton-up boys' image drew heavily from the military, dating back to World War II. The elaborately decorated jackets favored by the ton-up boys can be traced directly to the highly stylized and individualized A-20 flight jackets worn by bomber crews and fighter pilots during the second World War. Nose art, in which squadrons of pilots would decorate the fuselages of their aircraft with bold, brightly colored images of mascots, mythic creatures, pin-up art, or cartoons, was evident even during World War I; but by World War II, the form had reached a creative epoch.

American flight crews on weekend pass in British cities and villages cut dashing figures in their leather jackets, many covered in shoulder-to-shoulder pin-up art. The plane's nickname, often a clever play on words along the lines of "Hellzapoppin'," "FUGAWE Tribe," or "Hitler's Nightmare," would adorn a space just below the jacket's neckline while the lower panel was reserved for a formidable display of swastikas notating enemy planes the crew had shot down. Some bore miniature depictions of finned aerial

Kickstarting a café racer was equal parts necessity and highly dramatized ritual; open the fuel petcock, tickle the carbs, and find the elusive compression stroke...Simon Green

bombs to display the number of dangerous missions a particular crewmember had survived.

Half a decade after the war's end, café racers began wearing jackets adorned with similar markings, most decorated with snarling tigers, skulls, and crossbones or simply the brand name and engine size of their mount scrawled across the back in white household paint. It wasn't until a few years later, during the latter ton-up period of the mid- to late 1960s that riders really began embracing a pop-art approach to leather decoration, expressing a wry sense of humor in illustrations of television cartoon characters, popular sayings such as, "Wot! No Bike?" or the

Looking the business was never an easy job given the constant English rain; these rockers appear to need a dry towel and a warm cuppa! Author's collection

American biker movies played a strong role in the British motorcyclist's perception of himself. These 59 Club members display homemade Hells Angels jackets years before the notorious outlaw gang would surface in the U.K. Author's collection

Record Racing, the Rocker Era's Most Enduring Myth

Many legends surround the café racer cult and, like the lore of all subcultures, much of it is based in myth with a small sampling of reality thrown in for good measure. Take the much-reported practice of "record racing" for example. In nearly every mainstream media account of the rocker era of the 1960s, there's a mention of this practice, which involved selecting a favorite rock-and-roll 45-rpm record on a Wurlitzer juke box, and then having two café racer enthusiasts dash outside to a café's forecourt, where they'd manage to kick-start their motorcycles before sprinting into traffic for a race to a predetermined destination and back before the record ended. This was great theater to be sure, and if such practices were widespread, they were more than illustrative of the devil-may-care attitudes of the ton-up generation.

Record racing was forever cemented into the British public's imagination by a 1961 episode of the long-running police television program *Dixon of Dock Green*, entitled "The Burn-Up." Here, café racers were seen challenging each other to these mad, death-defying street races. When interviewed, however, most motorcyclists who frequented transport cafés during the early 1960s will admit they never heard of record racing until the *Dixon* episode aired. In reality, café racers rarely needed motivation for staging a multibike burn-up, and embarking on frequent, high-speed runs either to or between transport cafés was an essential part of a night behind the handlebars. Nevertheless, the legend was cemented into place as the British press, always eager to publish a sensational story regardless of its veracity, picked up and reported what it had seen on the telly as if it were verifiable truth.

Old-timers say that, in time, riders at some of the cafés may have attempted to stage brief street races within the rather stingy timeframe of a popular rock-and-roll song, but when placed under scrutiny, the act is nearly impossible to imagine. For one, the big singles and parallel twin engines popular during the rocker era were notoriously hard bastards to start. If record racing was a popular pastime, it's worth questioning how many of these contests were aborted or postponed while riders desperately hacked away at unresponsive kick starters. Likewise, with the average length of a pop song during the 1960s—whether we're talking Billie Davis's "Whatcha Gonna Do" or Gene Vincent's venerable "Be-Bop-A-Lula" clocking in at a modest three or four minutes from the opening chords to instrumental fade-out, these would have been some very short races indeed.

Some of the more interesting legends that survived from the café racer era do hold up to scrutiny. Veteran riders will tell of improbable street racing victories when riders aboard small, two-stroke twin Ariel Arrows would find themselves, with the assistance of a strong tailwind and judicious throttle application, catapulted to speeds well in excess of the homely little commuter bike's maximum velocity of just 80 miles per hour. There are horrific tales—riders being sliced into uniform-sized sections by falling into Britain's infamous traffic island barriers, for example—which are, unfortunately, true, backed up by newspaper accounts from the time. And whether the Beatles ever performed live at the Ace Café is still a claim that's debated rigorously among veteran rockers, and likely will be for generations to come.

infamous "Dodgy" and thumbs-down logo from *The Leatherboys.*

No less an authority on the café racer movement than Mark Wilsmore, proprietor of the Ace Café on London's North Circular Road, opines that the rocker look is a result of the jet age and fast motorcycles coinciding. "The rocker look, from the sheepskin-lined boots to the white-topped socks drawn over the black leather boot-tops, is all borrowed from the flyboys during World War II," he said. True enough, as the dashing, valiant fighter pilots who distinguished themselves during the Battle of Britain were known as Brylcreem Boys for their copious use of oil-based hair-dressing, a look emulated by rockers, Teddy Boys, and greasers a generation later.

Wilsmore contends that the technological marvels of jet propulsion so enthralled the British

Proudly displaying his 59 Club badges, this rider's multiple decades of membership in the youth charity offer instant street cred. Simon Green

The highly decorated rocker leathers were inspired by the U.S. Army Air Corps issue A20 flight jackets worn by American air crews during World War II. Simon Green

47

public during the Cold War years that youths from coast to coast demanded iconic designs like the Cromwell Jet helmet, which is closely, if not directly, styled to look like something worn by a Gloster Meteor pilot in the Royal Air Force. No rocker worth his weight in hair pomade would have hit the streets without an Everoak Racemaster helmet, worn by the cast members of *The Leatherboys* and still sought after on the vintage clothing market today. The stylistic link between rockers and pilots is best illustrated by both group's affinity for white silk scarves, which offer little in the way of protection from the elements but look damned dashing as they blow in the wind.

The sensation and appeal of speed was not only evident in the fashions favored by motorcyclists but also by the names and designs of the motorcycles they rode. BSA's Lightning and Golden Flash, Vincent's Comet, and the Velocette Thruxton were all inspired by speed in

name and intent, while their racy, swept-back lines appeared to have been designed by aircraft engineers. Surprisingly, and despite their reliance on and addiction to outright speed and racetrack handling, Wilsmore doesn't see Britain's superbike crowd as the rightful heirs to the café racer mantle.

"If you study how they mix motorcycles with military imagery and style, I'd say it was the streetfighter crowd who are the café racer's direct descendants," Wilsmore said. "The Roof helmets [ironically, perhaps, from France] they wear look like something a helicopter gunship pilot would wear in the skies over Afghanistan while the camouflage pants and nylon flight jackets are bought from military surplus shops. And they're really into customizing their machines for style and speed, which is exactly what the café racers did."

Today, show up at a rocker gathering and the baroque level or adornment seen on modern rockers is clearly miles beyond the often Spartan decor favored by the original ton-up boys. Jackets are frequently covered in badges, patches, and studs to the point where they resemble cowhide chain mail. They may look the dog's bollocks, so to speak, but old-timers will tell you that few, if any rockers could afford to bedeck their leathers

A fascinating still from an old BBC television chat show about British youth culture from the early 1960s; Teddy Boys and rockers take on their most formidable adversary: the viewing public. Author's collection

in such an extensive manner. Not only are these jackets overdone, they're impractical as well. The thought of being pierced by dozens of tiny pin-mounting spikes during a high-speed crash is almost too horrible to imagine.

But overdoing it is always in style, as evidenced by punk rockers who share a love of high leather fashion for shock value. During the 1970s, they would revisit the café racer's love of all things black and shiny, decorating their leathers with elaborate recreations of album cover art and illustrations from concert fliers. The common sight of punks wearing jackets with a length of chrome chain draped between the epaulets is a rocker style point resurrected twenty years hence, as is the current fad for wrapping one's face in a blue or red bandana, as seen among adherents to the recent rat rod scene.

Perhaps the clearest evidence that the café racer has cemented its place in the pop-style pantheon comes from a particular leather jacket, available from fashionable shops on London's King's Road in the 1990s. Adorned with a silkscreen of a massive 45-rpm record on the back and the image of rocker Eddie Cochran, the words *Rocker* and *Ton-Up Boy* had been carefully stenciled on each lapel. The leap from society's menace to fashion icon took only thirty years.

The rocker gear of yore may appear innocent and quaint, especially when viewed alongside today's multicolored, fully padded motorcycle leathers, but the boldness of the café racer look, coupled with the speed and aggression of the motorcycles, helped create an aura of romantic menace that lingers to this day. As former rocker Maria Barry explained, "The ton-up boys, as they would come to be known, were a clean-cut group compared to, say, the Hells Angels who were making the news in America at the same time. But you have to remember that England was a very different, less tolerant place in those days. You could get together with your mates for a burn-up, just having a laugh and enjoying the ride together, and you'd decided to stop somewhere for something to eat or drink, and half the people in the place would turn around and start staring. People would actually refuse to serve

A cover from Link, the 59 Club's monthly membership publication. Still in production today, Link, as its name implies provides contacts and resources for members. Author's collection

us or phone the police to get rid of us just because of the way we dressed."

The very term *café racer* was actually one of derision, meant to ridicule anyone who preferred to ride their motorcycle at breakneck speed from café to café rather on the track where the country's real two-wheeled heroes proved their mettle. Just as the term Promenade Percy had been coined to poke fun at an earlier generation of motorcycle speed merchants who preferred speed trials on the Brighton Promenade, café racer would come to be a title accepted by and worn with honor by the very people it had intended to offend.

These youthful riders were almost instantly caught up in the contradictions and social conflicts of a changing Britain, their reputations being perhaps the first and most lasting casualties. By the early 1960s, newspaper accounts of "Sawdust Caesars" and "Roadway Visigoths," as sociologist Stanley Cohen so expertly chronicled in *Folk Devils and Moral Panics*, (Paladin 1973) had some more gullible members of the public imagining that anyone on two-wheels was a switchblade-wielding dope addict and maybe even a Communist as well.

It must have been a tough time to be a motorcycle rider in Great Britain as it seemed every custom and pastime the café racers adopted out of necessity, the press either got completely wrong or misconstrued entirely. For example, the press characterized any gathering of motorcyclists as a gang or invading horde,

but rockers from the era describe events quite differently. Most say they tended to travel in groups of anywhere from two to twenty motorcycles not out of any innate need to harass or intimidate the motoring public, but because riding motorcycles was an inherently competitive sport. A pair of skilled, hotshot riders may have issued a friendly challenge to each other at one transport café or another, and as they mounted their machines and kicked them to life, word spread among the gathered that a real ring-dinger of a race was on. It was only natural to follow any competing riders to see the results of a particular burn-up for yourself, and if other riders chose to stretch a throttle cable to see whether they could keep up and pull a ton (English slang for reaching the speed of 100 miles per hour) or near about on their own machines, well, all the better.

"There was a definite camaraderie in riding together with your mates. There wasn't much

European 59 Club members roll in to the annual Rocker reunion en masse. Note the mix of vintage Davida Jet helmets and more modern gear. Simon Green

automobile traffic on the roads in those days and at night you pretty much had the roads to yourself. What few police vehicles were out tended to be slow little three-gear jobbies that did maybe 50 miles per hour at best and couldn't keep up with the slowest motorcycles in our group. But it was all harmless fun and we never set out to hurt anyone," said Dan Stuart of Luton, England, who still makes the annual pilgrimage to the Rocker Reunion at Brighton aboard his vintage Triumph Tiger 650.

It would, however, border on the disingenuous to suggest that all of the antics of the ton-up crowd were as harmless as a YWCA taffy-pull. These were

Café racer Australian style; this Triton Triple follows the mechanical template of the ton-up era so closely, it could easily be original. Greasy Kulture

Being seen on your café racer is nearly as much fun as a high-speed ride. Royal Enfield

A passion for fast motorbikes and rock-and-roll is often handed down from generation to generation as exemplified by this British Teddy Boy and his rocker son. Simon Green

excitable people in their teens and early adulthood, for the most part, who found themselves for the first time in charge of wondrously powerful, fast machines that, if pushed hard enough, could approach the sort of velocities previously known only to aircraft pilots or wealthy owners of speedboats. Teens can be notoriously overzealous drivers and their inexperience is almost always matched by an unnatural disregard toward bodily injury or death.

The rockers were no different as author and so-called "Ton-Up Chaplain" David Collyer recounts in *Double Zero*. When Collyer's group of café racer–mounted charges were evicted from a Sutton (southwest London suburb) coffee bar by locals who petitioned against the noise, smell, and general appearance of the rockers, they decided to provoke their neighbors with a bold display of group solidarity. The rockers, en masse, gathered outside the café where they offered Collyer a ride back to the youth center aboard one of a dozen or so motorcycles. Collyer, a tough fellow who survived half a decade with the often violent youth group, was nevertheless scared almost speechless as the pack of motorcycles hurtled, six-abreast, into the Smallbrook Ringway, a freshly paved section of dual carriageway located near the city center of Birmingham.

Though Collyer feared the rockers were taking him along for one of their famous "chicken runs" where they charged busy intersections against the traffic lights, daring their fellow riders to brake first, they instead charged headlong toward a trio of red, double-decker busses stopped at a traffic light. By timing their approach just right, the phalanx of speeding rockers managed to roar in between the busses at what Collyer described as "a tremendous speed," missing a multiple collision by a few inches at best. The brush with public transportation was close enough that the frazzled vicar recalls feeling a tugging sensation on his garments as he passed between the larger vehicles. Seems he had snagged his trousers on one of the passed buses.

Doubtless, events like these were considered little more than regular entertainment for the ton-up crowd. They may have hated the negative publicity

and added police attention such exploits brought them, but it's hard to imagine a cheeky, eighteen-year-old café racer not glowing, if only just a bit, at the thought that he was scaring half of England to death with his trusty motorbike. Regulars at coffee bars and cafés tell of hair-raising rides that were equally exhilarating and nerve-wracking; forcing your motorcycle up to the ton was a blast for sure, but that hurtling machine also had to stop quickly, which was just as challenging a feat. This was, after all, a time when the hydraulic disc brake was still a piece of expensive exotica found mostly on high-tech warplanes, not ordinary street bikes.

However fast a Norton Atlas or Triumph Tiger may have been to rev all the way to a ton-plus, stopping these hurtling, 450-pound missiles was a less precise affair. Unless tuned frequently and

expertly, even the most advanced, multi-leading shoe drum brakes from the likes of John Tickle or Grimeca (from Italy) were far from perfect, lacking both the precision stopping power and feedback at the lever of disc brakes. Rocker Ian Powell describes a particularly frightful ride during one Saturday night in 1967 that, fortunately for him, had a less-than tragic ending.

"A group of us (about twenty motorbikes) went to a few pubs but decided to come back to the local Red Lion. I was the first one back and

Café Chronicles

Unlike the chopper movement that swept through the U.S. motorcycling scene at roughly the same time, café racers never spawned the level of media interest as choppers. The exploits of mods and rockers might have made for exciting tabloid newspaper fodder, but the stripped-down, racetrack-inspired motorcycles favored by leather-jacketed 1960s bikers have somehow escaped the media's imagination. This has proven, in time, to be both a blessing and a curse; unlike choppers, café racers are yet to be condemned to status as a rich man's plaything.

The café racer scenes, on both sides of the Atlantic, have mercifully escaped the codified uniforms and middle-aged, outlaw biker play-acting of the custom Harley scene, lending it a freshness and validity rare among motorsports subcultures over a half century old. Show up at a motorcycle gathering on a chopper, and it's likely you'll be mistaken for a wealthy orthodontist harboring latent Sonny Barger fantasies. Arrive at the same event on a café racer, and half the crowd will scratch their heads in confusion as to the machine's make and model while just as many will have little clue as to the purpose and appeal of a low-slung, vintage racing bike. However, that's a sword that cuts both ways as the lack of a comprehensive chronicle of the café racer era has frustrated many an enthusiast.

From the off, café racers with their ritualistic nighttime burn-ups and rakish image seemed ripe pickings for the film industry, but to date, few directors have acknowledged the appeal of fast motorbikes on screen. Among the best-known café racer films was director Sidney Furie's 1964 *The Leatherboys*. Shot on location at London's Ace Café and on roads between the British capital and Scotland (and in the depths of winter, no less), *The Leatherboys* is a fascinating, if sometimes turgid, take on working-class romance and identity crises set among the rocker set. Because the film's central plotline focused more on a young Triumph rider's marital woes than the rocker scene per se, many café racer purists have complained that *The Leatherboys* was more soap opera than ton-up travelogue.

A scene from Sidney Furie's The Leatherboys *one of the only feature-length films produced about the ton-up generation.* Author's collection

A group of troubled teenage café racers are the focal point of *Some People*, a sometimes amateurish but enjoyable film from 1963. This time, the motorcyclists, replete in their black leather jackets and shiny, open-faced Jet helmets, must choose between a life of breaking traffic laws and brawling, or preparing for their futures under a Duke of Edinburgh job-training scheme. It doesn't take a Francis Ford Coppola to see which direction this film would take.

The brilliant film actor Oliver Reed lent his smoldering presence to a silly science-fiction rocker flick *These Are the Damned* in 1961, which played on both society's fears of unruly, motorcycle riding youth and nuclear proliferation.

Rockers made a brief appearance in director Ken Loach's 1968 *Up the Junction*, a gritty, realistic take on urban social problems that telegraphed Loach's later approach to filmmaking.

In 1979, rock giants The Who brought a big-budget screen adaptation of their concept album *Quadrophenia* to life, creating perhaps the most realistic and socially relevant take on the rocker era. Graced with a brilliant musical soundtrack and offering a bird's-eye view of the identity crises, youthful rebellion, and personal costs of the mods vs. rockers era—from a decidedly mod point of view, that is—*Quadrophenia* is a standout for café racer fans and movie buffs alike.

David Hemmings in Some People *a 1964 release chronicling the lives of Bristol-based rockers whose nightly burn-ups land them in trouble with the law.* Author's collection

Actress Rita Tushingham, star of The Leatherboys *outfitted in her Jet helmet and Belstaff waterproofs during filming in 1963.* Author's collection

Thankfully, the literary arts have been more kind to the café racer era, providing some excellent, if difficult to find, reading on the subject. British writer and rock music impresario Johnny Stuart's *Rockers* (Plexus 1987) was a lavishly illustrated, well-written account of all things that shook, rattled, and rolled during the 1950s and 1960s, starting at the dawn of the BSA Gold Star era and running a greasy link straight through to the post-punk days of the Clash, skinheads, and the Chelsea Bridge rocker reunions of the 1980s.

An altogether more technical take on the era was provided in vivid detail in Mike Clay's *Café Racers* (Osprey 1988). With its effortless verbiage, fascinating period images (some of the shots of early café racer hybrids and group rides are truly amazing), and knowledgeable take on the subject, Clay's book has since become a sought-after collector's item, fetching up to $300.00 U.S. on internet auction house eBay.

The early 1990s saw renowned British motorcycle writer Mick Walker compile two pithy though comprehensive volumes on the café racer, *Café Racers of the 1960s* and *Superbike Specials of the 1970s* (Windrow & Greene 1994). The latter revealed the engineering and technological links between those Featherbed-framed twins from the rocker era and the faster-than-a-speeding-bullet (but poor-cornering) Japanese superbikes from a decade later.

For the most accurate, hands-on view of what life was like for a ton-up boy at the height of the café racer craze, look no further than David Collyer's *Double Zero* (Fontana 1973). Long out of print (but available on out-of-print booksellers sites), Collyer's gripping true-life chronicle of his five years spent as a vicar and youth charity volunteer in a working-class section of Birmingham, is a screenwriter's dream come true. Gone are any romantic, swashbuckling notions of riding with the rockers, replaced by the petty violence, vicious rivalries, and the sometimes exhilarating, often terrifying world of high-speed runs in greasy, pitch-black streets. Few writers have captured the tenor of a time as thoroughly and as confidently as Collyer, and it's a shame no one has capitalized on his experiences in the years since.

when some of the others got back they told me George and Big S had gone through a five-bar gate at 80 miles per hour, trying to avoid the police. When George and Big S arrived they were covered in soil and told us what happened. When they saw the police they turned around and took a narrow side road that was a quarter-mile straight followed by a 90-degree left hand bend at the end. They didn't know this route too well and went into the gate at the end of the straight. George went through the gate; luckily it was an old wooden one, so when George hit it with his Bonneville (Big S was riding pillion) he went straight through into the field. When Big S saw George he thought he was dead or badly injured and didn't want to move him, but George got up with no broken bones. The field had just been ploughed so the only damage was a broken headlight and wounded pride. Many times after this when we went out George was told not to gate crash," Powell said.

Read enough on the café racer era, and stories of riders who met their fate because of motorcycles that failed to stop at intersections (or slow for curves, or avoid kissing the bumper of a bus or truck, and so on) or while trying to avoid the Plod or Old Bill, as police constables were affectionately called in those days, are painfully common. Tales abound of motorcycles revved until their innards erupted in showers of splintered metal, which, in retrospect, only added to the café racer's hairy-chested allure. With all the mechanized mayhem, it's a wonder so many café racers survived to tell their tales. One such rider, former rocker Dan Stuart, described the era as one of chaos and fun on the roads made possible by unprecedented economic opportunity. Britain, was, after all, rebuilding itself after six years of war—and lots of new experiences. Mostly, his days were spent working in order

to meet the weekly obligations of his beloved Triumph Tiger, which commanded most of his daylight hours and those of his mates.

"People claimed [rockers] rode mostly under cover of night because we were up to something, but to be honest, we'd worked all day and were in desperate need of recreation. We'd sometimes get together for a ride and end up staying on the roads until almost daybreak. We'd ride from Café Rising Sun in Kent, all the way up to the Busy Bee for a coffee, and then, if we still had it in us, we'd make a run to the Ace in London before heading straight back to work. We were young then so that wasn't really a problem," laughed Stuart at the memory. This goes a long way toward understanding why the café racer movement was often (mis) characterized in the press as some sort of dark, nocturnal cult whose crimes were best committed under cover of darkness.

With so much negative press aimed at not only motorcyclists but at youth in general, it is no surprise that, in 1962, Father Bill Shergold, a mild-mannered vicar, formed the 59 Club youth charity, which provided not only constructive charity work but a place to kill off-bike hours and a collective sense of purpose for many a bike-mad British youth. Based in the Hackney section of northeast London, and later, relocating to nearby Plaistow, the 59 Club was actually launched in 1959, but it took three more years for Shergold to open a special section for bikers.

A likeable pastor who enjoyed motorcycling on his Triumph Speed Twin, Shergold was familiar with the mobs of leather-jacketed rockers who tore up the city's arterial roads. Charged with the mission of giving the kids a place to go of their own, he wrote a letter published in *The Motorcycle* which led him to the local Triumph Owner's Club and later to the notorious Ace Café. Shergold would later acknowledge being frightened silly before approaching the Ace's noisy, smoky forecourt and riding past the crowded car park twice before deciding to go inside. But after working up the courage to make his way inside, the vicar found himself facing a crowd all too desperate for his kind of tough love.

In a matter of months, the newly launched 59 Club could boast a membership well into the hundreds, each identified by the distinctive, black,

The ton-up cult spreads worldwide as evidenced by this photo depicting rockers from six countries and as many different nationalities. Simon Green

Triumph Thunderbird with "bathtub" rear wheel enclosure looks cooler today than when Marlon Brando rode a similar model in The Wild One. Author's collection

"I think they were so tickled that a clergyman would be interested in them, but I always took them seriously. Their parents didn't, their teachers didn't, but I did," Shergold told an interviewer in 1990. For more than thirty-five years Shergold held court at the 59 Club, which still operates after moving its headquarters to a new location in nearby Dorking back in 1995.

Shergold's warm embrace by these societal outcasts was similar to what author David Collyer would later experience with his Double Zero Youth Trust. Where Shergold, having been the first riding vicar to be recognized for reaching out to the rockers, received an amazing—and, it must be noted, fully warranted—amount of press, Collyer's exploits were covered rarely, except for a long-lost BBC documentary film from 1967. It's no surprise that

round shoulder patch that's still sought after by motorcyclists everywhere. The club's twice-weekly meetings brought in cyclists from throughout the British Isles, who helped organize massive group rides, stage charity fund-raising events, and even operate a recovery vehicle to pick-up stranded riders. A monthly membership magazine, *Link*, is still in production with collectors offering top dollar for copies produced during the early 1960s. A canny self-promoter, "The Revvin' Rev," as he was known, had the ability to play to the news cameras whenever a gang of rockers delivered shoes to a needy orphanage or when a comment was needed to offset tales of misguided youth.

Mark Wilsmore, the man behind the re-launch of London's fabled Ace Café, prepares to lead some 50,000 rockers for the annual Southend Shakedown ride. Simon Green

the café racers flocked to these like-minded authority figures; after being shunned by their parents in many cases, thrown out of countless cafés and coffee bars, accused of everything short of a war crime by the media, and forced to endure inconsiderate, and at times, purely homicidal car drivers, finding a place to share with fellow motorcyclists must have seemed just this side of paradise.

Collyer's working-class café racers were so desperate for a home away from their often dismal homes, some 150 motorcycles filled his parish parking lot on a typical Christmas night. Years later, those numbers would swell to nearly 500, revealing just how popular motorcycles were during the café racer era, and how unpopular it must have been to count one's self among their ranks.

In the end, it's safe to say the rockers have the last laugh. Despite how the media portrayed café racers—as misfits, outcasts, and law-breakers—the rocker cult continues to grow, some fifty years later. café racers were even chosen as the subject of "The Wild Ones," a well-received gallery show at London's Brent Museum in the fall of 2007, proving that speed, sound, and style are far from a fad.

3

Café Racer Scene

There has long been the cult of the café racer in the United States, though it has existed far outside the motorcycle mainstream. As early as 1973, *Motorcyclist* magazine, one of the country's most widely read two-wheeled publications, featured a collection of customized streetbikes in an all café-racer issue, though the resultant aftermarket café craze that many predicted failed to materialize. This can be attributed to the all-powerful allure of the chopper and custom-cruiser motorcycles in America, a place where high-performance motoring was, for many years, the sole provenance of automobile drivers.

Growing up, I remember seeing sleek Japanese motorcycles adorned with tiny, bikini fairings, rocket-shaped tail sections, and flat, drag-style handlebars; but this was simply how Kawasaki and Honda designed their high-performance streetbikes at the time. The men who rode these machines, at least in my area, did not do so because they evoked images of Dunstall Nortons and Dave Degens's Dresdas, but because they offered cheap, exhilarating transportation. Looking back on the streetbikes and riders from my childhood in the 1970s, some of the African-American

From the start, the nightly adventures of the ton-up boys provided ample headline fodder for Britain's tabloids—sensationalism helped foster the image of the rocker as a lawless hooligan alive with the public. Author's collection

motorcycle clubs popular at the time bore a distinct stylistic similarity to British rockers from twenty years earlier; both groups favored the head-down, bum-in-the-air riding style essential for fast street riding.

I find it curious that black, inner-city U.S. motorcycle clubs like the Zulus and Afro Dogs dressed in nearly the same style of ornately studded, tight-fitting black leathers that the rockers had during the 1960s. Both groups valued speed, camaraderie, and riding skill above nearly everything else, and there have been times when I've stood among a group of British rockers as they obsessively discuss cam timing and carb rejetting and I could swear I'm back on Brushton Avenue, in my hometown, hanging out with the Zulus on a Friday night. Call it coincidence, the universal language of speed or the inevitable spread of cultural influences, but it is fascinating to find parallels between riders of such different stripes.

While untold tens of thousands of Americans rode and raced Japanese inline four factory café racers during the 1970s, the British café racer movement in this country, until very recently, has been largely relegated to the restoration of vintage bikes, less the cultural movement seen overseas. Publications such as *Walneck's Classic Cycle Trader*, a long-running monthly, caters to the vintage restoration crowd and regulars of the various concours d'elegance motorcycle shows. With its weird habit of running ads for motorcycles that have sold months previously and reprints of features stories and road tests from long-defunct enthusiast magazines, *Walneck's* offers an odd, captivating portal into the U.S. café racer scene as it were.

To spot a Manx Norton, Triton, or Egli-Vincent on these shores means traveling to one of the many well-attended vintage gatherings held around the country. Places like the Peoria TT held in Illinois, the pits at Daytona's Speedway early in Bike Week in March, or the American Motorcyclist Association's Vintage Grand Prix, now called Vintage Motorcycle Days, at the Mid-Ohio Sports Car Course are all well populated with café racers. Most of the owners are middle-

aged or older, and their machines are generally trailered to the events, arriving in a fresher-than-showroom condition that reflects the considerable wealth and advanced age of the average American café racer enthusiast.

My first real visceral evidence that a viable, energetic American café racer scene was emerging came at the Vintage Grand Prix when I spotted a group of youthful racers in the Mid-Ohio paddock. Dressed in a rag-tag collection of vintage, all-black racing leathers and modern, multicolored one-piece track gear, these blokes' motorcycles were a funky collection of café racers and vintage track bikes, their bullet-shaped vintage fairings evoking images of TT paddocks from the 1960s. The oldest of the group couldn't have been older than midtwenties and each rider and machine

wore a distinctive oval-shaped logo reading, "Fuel Café: Milwaukee."

Introducing myself, I soon struck up a conversation with Scott Johnson, a café racer–mad roadracer who also owned Fuel Café, a hip, off-beat little coffee shop in Milwaukee's Riverwest neighborhood. Johnson possessed an encyclopedic knowledge of café racers, riffing on the accomplishments of the Manx Norton and the best gear ratios for Triumph Bonnevilles with the authority of someone far older. Johnson was not only sponsoring a race team comprised of customers from his coffee shop, he was among the riders, piloting both a Honda CB450 roadracer and a Kawasaki 650 four-powered sidecar rig in the American Historic Racing Motorcycle Association championships.

The Fuel Café crew wasn't just satisfied sitting around the café sipping espressos and talking shop: Johnson and crew were determined to replicate the balls-to-the-wall riding style of the rockers to

Italian café racers are at their best on the tight, serpentine roads of Europe where torquey engines and sharp handling come together for two-wheeled bliss. Ducati Motor Holdings S.p.A.

its fullest extent, staging some well-known and notorious road rallies during the 1990s. Their annual Frozen Snot ride was held each year on New Year's Day and challenged riders to a 100-mile circuit on Milwaukee's icy streets, regardless of the weather.

Next came the Fuel Café TT an annual "race" staged on public roads that was something of a cross between the Isle of Man TT and the Gumball Rally for cars. Tales abound of riders pushing their machines well past the posted limits during the feverish 140-mile race, which eventually attracted both serious roadracers and the attentions of local police. The event

was stopped after the mayhem and legend grew completely out of hand, but the Fuel Café's reputation as America's foremost café racer hangout was firmly in place.

Fuel Café was not the first post-modern take on the café racer scene to emerge in the states. In 1997, Chicago native and motorcycle enthusiast Larry Fletcher opened the Ace Café Chicago in the Windy City, catering to a clientele that Fletcher described as "urban vintage riders." Though Fletcher was far too young to have ever visited the original Ace Café during its heyday, he had studied the rocker scene religiously, imbuing his tasteful, well-designed café with a style that paid tribute to the transport café of yore. The Ace Café Chicago's decor was decidedly more upscale than the well-worn Formica and grease-stained plastic interiors of places like the Busy Bee, with

vintage movie posters and a massive 59 Club logo illuminated in the front window. Granted, most Chicago bikers wouldn't know a rocker from a rocker arm, but the Ace Chicago was popular, receiving a brief write-up in England's *Classic Bike* magazine at a time when the original Ace Café was still a tire depot.

There was a certain charm to the place: The menus featured cleverly worded items like "The Hailwood Ham Sandwich," for example, and the bar area sported an authentic red cast iron British telephone box, with a Triumph Tiger twin mounted above. Best of all, a steady clientele of Britbike enthusiasts frequented the Ace Café

Rebirth of the Rockers

Though the brief and very local rocker reunion movement that swept Britain during the late 1970s waned throughout the next decade and a half, in 1994 the movement received what was to be its biggest boost yet. That's when a former mounted police constable from the North London neighborhood of Stonebridge decided to issue a call that would forever change the café racer movement. Mark Wilsmore has long admired and researched the café racer era, fascinated, he would later explain, "by its inherent, unique Britishness. The Americans have the whole Harley-Davidson thing and that way of life, but when you look to the history behind why people love fast motorcycles and the style that comes with them, well, that's uniquely British and all draws from the rocker tradition."

Wilsmore's words would prove prophetic in the summer of 1994 when he announced plans to host a nationwide rocker reunion rally at the site of the Ace, perhaps the most famous of all the transport cafés popular during the ton-up era. The Ace closed in 1969, victim to a changing Britain more accustomed to grabbing quick, on-the-go food at a Little Chef than a greasy café full of loud motorcyclists. But much to his surprise, some 10,000 riders showed up at the Ace, by then a tire-changing shop, to celebrate this "unique Britishness."

Captured in the remarkable documentary film *An Ace Day*, the event saw motorcycles of every variety parked along London's North Circular road for miles, while many tearful, unexpected personal reunions occurred, with former ton-up boys meeting mates they'd lost track of back when long sideburns were popular the first time around.

Crowds were hungry for a hallowed café racer site, as veterans of the Busy Bee Café in nearby Watford had been gathering on the site, now occupied by a hotel, since just after the airy, modern-looking restaurant was leveled in 1970.

A keen observer of history, Wilsmore announced to the gathered his plans to purchase the old Ace Café building and restore it to its former glory. By 2001, despite encountering miles of bureaucratic red tape and a devastating flood caused by a ruptured water main, Wilsmore's dream for a café racer Mecca prevailed. Today, the Ace Café stands as a living, roaring, high-octane tribute to all things fast and undeniably cool in that inimitable café racer manner. The interior of the café, first opened in 1938, has been restored to closely resemble its look from a half century past. The Ace's trademark spades logo on a checkerboard background decorates the floors and walls, and the original front wall of removable glass doors has again been designed to open on warm nights, letting the sound of motorbike engines and the smell of Castrol R mingle with chip grease and the sounds of rock-and-roll.

Today, there is a full schedule of motorcycling events taking place at the Ace, serving not only café racer enthusiasts but hot-rodders, street fighters, and even mods on their garishly decorated scooters. And best of all, having the most fabled of café racer hangouts back in operation means riding a café racer is a far less lonely experience than it once was.

Chicago during its brief, two-year run, proving that American bikers were interested in speed as well as style. In fact, in more recent years, the Ace Café Chicago has proven prophetic as Chicago is now home to one of several ton-up clubs operating around the United States. And not only has Larry Fletcher's original Ace Café Chicago become an integral part of local motorcycle lore, a "Rocker reunion" run is staged from Delilah's Bar, a popular café racer hangout, back to the site of the Ace Chicago which, like most vacant retail space in this nation, has become a Starbucks.

Unlike the many patch clubs that operate in many larger American cities, the ton-up clubs are not interested in intimidating other bikers, capitalizing on the methamphetamine trade, or staging public shoot-outs with their rivals. Instead, they're comprised of mostly under forty-year-olds who, like their namesakes, enjoy the camaraderie and thrills of building and riding fast motorbikes.

That's the primary motivation behind the formation in 2004 of the Brit Iron Rebels, a nationwide café racer club established by California rock musician Rikki Rockett. According to club officer Armand Ensanian, Rockett's vision was to form "a worldwide group of individuals focused on the preservation, restoration, and promotion of true classic and retro-styled British motorcycles. Keeping in contact via internet chat rooms and discussion boards, the club has since spread to ten countries and stages several events each year.

"The club is based on the retro style of the rockers of the fifties and sixties in Great Britain and our membership encompasses all classic and retro British motorcycle enthusiasts: the collector, the purist, the racer, and radical customizer," he explained.

The Brit Iron Rebels are a media-savvy bunch, working to produce a film, titled *Brittown*, that chronicles the rapid ascendancy of the vintage café racer scene in the United States. "The historic ties we seek include the rocker hooligan café racers of the fifties and sixties as well as the glory days of British racing. Additionally, it is a forum for builders of radical custom British bikes and restorers of the classics," he said.

Now that the term *British motorcycle enthusiast* no longer refers solely to white-haired concourse junkies and wealthy vehicle collectors, clubs like this are comprised of an interesting mixture of ages, sexes, and races. Rockett described it as a collection of "older folks looking to capture that snapshot of our carefree days and younger members seeking an identity that is much more unique than the countless 'me-too' biker clubs.

"To many of us baby boomers, vintage British bikes were not always vintage. They are

"Hey, man, can I borrow your Brylcreem?" Rocker Steve Carpenter test-rides a clean, Dunstall Honda CB750. Aaron Hollebecke

the bikes we know best," Rockett said. "We dreamt of owning one when we were fourteen and bought one when we were nineteen. They were affordable, light, and fast. They were modern compared to Harleys and Indians and easily converted to off-road applications. The attraction today is based on reliving that. We put on a Davida helmet and goggles, and we are once again nineteen, dragging our heels with cleats sparking in the night, looking for that girl

Winding roads and a well-wound throttle, two elements of the café racer cult that will never go out of style. Aaron Hollebecke

to hop on the back. This is the very same magic that attracts the younger enthusiasts as well. They envy the era of the cigarette-smoking café-racing bad boy, screaming down the cobbled streets of London or bragging about breaking the ton.

"However, there is another segment of enthusiasts: the kid whose dad owned a Triumph. He remembers those magic moments on a Sunday morning riding down the back roads, holding on to Dad, wind blowing in the ears because that helmet never did fit right."

Talk to the modern café enthusiasts and they'll make frequent references to what they see as a cultural spiritual bankruptcy in the custom cruiser scene. What was once specialized and custom has become common, many say, especially at a time when choppers are produced on assembly lines and there is seldom a kinetic side to owning one, as many choppers spend their lives parked in massive, three-stall garages or ferried to custom motorcycle shows in enclosed trailers. Instead, the experience of riding a vintage café racer is a far more involved experience with a level of commitment—financial and physical—required to maintain a vintage motorcycle on modern roads.

The best part of being in a modern rocker club is how other motorcyclists tend to realize that we can be cool in any crowd, said Ensanian, who can count riders of modern superbikes and Harley types among the Brit Iron Rebel's supporters. "Those of us who rode Triumph T120s, Norton Commandos, and 750 Hondas were content with their power and versatility; but when we tried to keep up with the newer machines, most of us could not. So we looked into the past where we're satisfied with the speed, handling, and sound that give us thrills. We also are not obligated to race every bike that pulls alongside because everyone knows you just can't ride a GSX-R slow. But take that Dominator with the clip-ons out and no one will think ill of you for not smoking the tires. You look and feel like you're going fast," said Ensanian, who rides and maintains a 1956 BSA Gold Star.

Café racers do offer a remarkable connection between rider and machine. Intrinsically Spartan, the bike's every vibration and engine pulse is felt through the wrists, groin, and ankles. The seating position is uncomfortable, and the bars far too low for anything but quick short jaunts, but owning a café racer, especially a vintage one, requires mechanical skill that was a prerequisite to motorcycling a long time ago. That in itself is a real departure from the impersonal, new-bike-every-year ethos of modern performance motorcycles.

Some of the larger modern ton-up clubs can count memberships well into the high two figures, with New Jersey, Florida, and Texas supporting

some of the most active. Most stage several annual rides and meets, arriving in an impressive pack to rockabilly concerts, vintage motorcycle shows, and the like. Unlike rocker and café racer clubs in, say, Japan, the stateside ton-up clubs embrace a far more relaxed approach to the café era, riding a collection of all sorts of machines from BMWs to sport tourers and the ubiquitous Harley-Davidsons. Likewise, their mode of dress is a mixture of greaser, rocker, and wear-what-you-will casualness. For anyone who has ever been asked to leave a British rock-and-roll club for wearing modern trainers, this is a welcome relief. It stands in direct contrast to the almost religious dedication to period-perfect style evident in Japanese ton-up clubs, however.

When the 59 Club meets in Tokyo, members have spent weeks, and many thousands of yen, affecting a look that approximates the rocker era in its most minute detail. No minutiae from the

A group of German streetfighter fans kick back at the Ace after a 400-mile ride across Europe. Massive nightly crowds and a regular schedule of events have kept the Ace hopping. Simon Green

Ton-up art adorns the iron gates adjacent to the Ace Café, Stonebridge Park, London. The overpass has been the place where motorcyclists have enjoyed the echo of their own exhausts before a North London burn-up since 1939. Simon Green

Opposite page: Rev'em up and go as a group of restored café racers line up for a group ride. Increased traffic in London means your skills had better be as sharp as your throttle hand. Simon Green

1960s is spared, from the inch-perfect placement of a cherished 59 Club arm patch to the level of blinding polish on the engine cases of a restored BSA Spitfire. The regimented style is so important here that retro café racers in Japan will pay the equivalent of several hundred U.S. dollars for the prestige of owning a tiny key chain ornament once distributed by Esso gas stations during the rocker period: The tiny oil-drip figurines were once as common in England as chip-grease stains, but they are now revered icons.

Likewise, Japanese rockers I've met at rallies say the expense and mechanical expertise involved in owning and operating a genuine classic British café racer overseas translates into some serious status in the Asian rocker scene. Riders aboard genuine Tritons, for instance, will find themselves riding up front of the pack to a 59 Club Tokyo gathering, while those favoring café racers powered by modern Japanese-engined motorcycles will be accepted but without the prestige of a real vintage bike. Nevertheless, it is amazing to witness the ingenuity and DIY spirit employed by Japanese café racers as they fashion impressive replicas of vintage café bikes from late-model Japanese iron.

A common donor bike is Yamaha's 500cc SR single. Produced in large quantities from 1979 until the early 1990s, the punchy little kick-start single is an endlessly adaptable template for custom builders. With an aftermarket gas tank or a change of front brake and paint, the SR500 can pass at a glance for a Matchless G50 racer, an AJS CSR or, at an even quicker glance, a Manx

Norton. This is the one place where Honda's ill-fated GN500 from the early 1990s is a highly desirable motorcycle, it too lending itself to café custom tricks rather easily. Talking to Japanese rockers at the Ace and other British events, they speak reverently of a "golden age of motorcycles" and lament not having been around for the original rocker movement.

With their highly regimented society, most of the Asian rockers tend to wear their gear only during weekend gatherings or at special rock-and-roll–theme events so as not to offend their peers. For many of these riders, the café racer provides an alter-ego, a secret identity and admission into a world where only an appreciation of speed—and the bonds of friendship that it can create—is all that matters.

Out on the West Coast of the United States, where fashion seldom includes such feverish adherence to code, riders with a variety

A pair of typical American café racers, circa early twenty-first century. Built at Milwaukee's The Shop from salvaged Honda CB350 and 450 twins, motorcycles like these are attracting a new generation of riders to the ton-up fold. Author's collection

of motorcycles have gathered for decades at the Rock Store, California's oldest-running weekend motorcycle hangout. Located on Mulholland Highway in the scenic hills just north of Los Angeles and east of Malibu, the Rock Store serves as a stop for the annual Giro d'California rally, a re-creation of Italy's most famous motorcycle road race, staged by a group of vintage bike–mounted Californians with a well-developed sense of café racer history.

Farther north, in San Francisco, the Zeitgeist Bar has a steady clientele of performance-minded motorcyclists, drawing in the few vintage and modern café racers who call the hilly city by the bay home. Zeitgeist saw some fierce competition for the San Francisco biker trade when the Ace Café San

Twilight of the Ton-up Boys

As the brilliant sociologist and motorcycle enthusiast Maz Harris observed in his book *Biker* (Faber and Faber 1985) the original era of the ton-up boy and the café racer came to an unceremonious halt in the late 1960s when the American chopper flick *Easyrider* opened at the Odeon Cinema in London's Leicester Square. One look at the film's irreverent anti-heroes, Captain America (Peter Fonda) and Billy (a spacey, hopped-up Dennis Hopper), in their fringed leathers and mile-long Harley-Davidson choppers, and the very idea of blasting down the M25 with your bum in the air and your gloved hands gripping a set of clip-on handlebars mounted somewhere just north of the front wheel spindle suddenly seemed like some sort of cruel joke.

This was the Age of Aquarius, after all, a time when free love, mind-expanding pharmaceuticals, and do-your-own-thing social relativism were in. Dressing up like Gene Vincent and bopping along on a motorcycle that looked as if John Surtees might have raced it at Brands Hatch in 1955 was simply not the done thing. But regardless of pop culture's image-makers' disregard of the café racer cult, adherents to the cause were not to be deterred.

During the "wilderness years" of the 1970s, many café racer purists and backstreet engineers, who had been crafting high-performance motorcycles since the 1950s, felt vindicated by the Japanese manufacturers who had obviously admired their designs from afar. Every manufacturer, from Yamaha with its Triumph-clone TX750 and XS650s to Kawasaki with its W650, which was little more than a carbon-copy BSA Lightning, had emulated the best of Britain as best they could. As the decade progressed, Kawasaki's 130-mile-per-hour Z1 followed styling cues borrowed almost directly from café racer specials builders like Paul Dunstall and Fritz Egli. With the British motorcycle industry finally succumbing to its extended death rattle when Triumph bit the dust in 1982, most café racer enthusiasts had already abandoned the Union Jack for faster, more reliable Japanese production bikes that in style, performance, and purpose were café racers at heart.

Naturally, not all of the original ton-up riders abandoned their British motorcycles entirely. Most, it seemed, eagerly accepted the domination of the ubiquitous Japanese four-cylinder superbikes and their breathtaking performance; but hidden in the rear of many a garden shed was a beloved old Norton Atlas or BSA Goldie, replete with megaphone silencers and Taylor-Dow piston kit. The rockers may have embraced Gary Glitter and the cassette tape recorder, but their hearts were still with the traditional rock-and-roll DJs who never forgot the importance of "Three Steps to Heaven" and "20 Flight Rock."

The original rocker reunions were held along the Chelsea Bridge, the river Thames, separating Battersea and Chelsea and the rest of Central London and are largely credited to Les Paterson, an old-school rocker who operates the Gear Head Shop in the British capital. Paterson helped organize subsequent events held each January at the Battersea Town Hall, which ran until 1999 when a fatal stabbing between members of outlaw biker clubs forced cancellation. Still, Paterson's work reconnecting the old ton-up crowd and drawing in a new generation of rockers was a siren call of sorts that's still being answered.

Paterson's events might have appeared to have materialized out of thin air, but the throngs of vintage café racers, their riders bedecked in studded leathers and wearing the telltale shoulder patches of veteran café racers: Johnson's café in Kent, the Ace, and the Busy Bee had never really gone anywhere. Motorcyclists had been gathering on the Chelsea Bridge since just after World War II and the weekly Friday-night gatherings soon became de rigueur for the café racer set, whether it was a wind-blown veteran of a thousand burn-ups or a newly minted neo-rocker astride a restored Triton.

The initial rocker reunion of the late 1970s also coincided with a reawakening of the traditional rock-and-roll scene in Great Britain. By the early 1980s, performers as diverse as the Elvis-worshiping Shakin' Stevens, Crazy Cavan and his Rhythm Rockers, and even mainstream rocker Nick Lowe had made rock-and-roll—or as we Yanks called it, rockabilly—not only popular, but downright cool again.

Francisco opened in 1999. The venue was decorated with a collection of vintage British motorcycling memorabilia and hosted a series of roots rock concerts and vied with nearby Zeitgeist for clientele, but was short-lived and closed after only two years in operation. Recently, the Ace Café San Francisco reopened under new ownership as a more contemporary motorcyclist's meeting place, offering a steady supply of roadracing broadcasts on its multiple TV screens, though whether it manages to attract genuine café motorcyclists or just rockabillies and hipsters who dress like rockers is anyone's guess.

Where these cafés shine is in staging events, which seem to draw out well-hidden café motorcycles seldom seen on American streets. A few years after meeting Fuel Café's Scott Johnson, he invited me to attend an event at his coffee shop, a celebration of what he called "all the motorcycles that aren't Harley-Davidsons." Growing up in the shadow of

America's most famous motorcycle manufacturer has left many Generation X bikers in that town with an irreverent take on the sport; as a result, they'll ride basically anything not made in Milwaukee. So when Harley-Davidson Motor Company staged a one hundredth anniversary homecoming rally in 2003, attracting hundreds of thousands of the faithful, Johnson, along with a café racer enthusiast pal Scott Radke, organized a counter-event that became known as Rockerbox. The day-long gathering brought out a demographic conspicuously absent from mainstream motorcycle events in the United States: young people, most of whom prefer to customize their motorcycles rather than purchase new machines from showrooms.

The preferred aesthetic at Rockerbox is the café racer, with some impressive, inventive machines in evidence. There were Norton Commandos, Triumphs by the score, and a few Yamaha SR500 singles modified to resemble Manx Nortons. Moto Guzzi Le Mans café racers are still available for a few thousand bucks, tops, in the Midwest, and a few Rockerbox regulars

Larry Fletcher, proprietor of the brilliant but short-lived Ace Café, Chicago. An offshoot Ace Café also operates in San Francisco. Kim Love

Japanese café redux—considered a pale imitation of the classic British parallel twin when introduced in 1971—Yamaha's XS650 has since become a café racer classic in its own right. Simon Green

Running out of gas is still a problem, even for pretty girl rockers. Simon Green

Veteran of one thousand burn-ups, 1960s rocker Ian Stuart was a regular at the Busy Bee Café in Watford. He still rides a Triumph. Simon Green

seemed intent on outfitting theirs with stunning, 6-gallon aluminum gas tanks and thundering sweptback exhausts. Most of the attendees wore the grungy look familiar to artists and punk rockers everywhere, and their machines were an equally outrageous collection of low-buck rat-rod choppers, matte-black, street-fighter late-model Japanese sportbikes, and homemade café racers built from CB350 and 400 Supersport Hondas.

With a large Ace Café logo on my own leathers, I attracted a crowd of eager questions

during my visit to Rockerbox. They wanted to know how they could get their hands on the parts necessary to build a BSA Gold Star or a Triton of their own, and they were curious as to whether there were still ton-up boys risking it all on the streets of Great Britain. It was a line of questioning I'd hear often over the next few years as a nascent café racer resurgence began to attract the attention of a growing number of twenty- and thirty-something riders. Many were exposed to the rocker scene through articles published in

small-circulation glossies like the excellent *Dice*, originally published in the U.K., and *The Horse* a traditional outlaw chopper publication based in Michigan, that suddenly, inexplicably opened its pages to café racers a few years ago.

With choppers relegated to their status as barely ridden, high-dollar rich men's toys, many youthful custom motorcycle enthusiasts wanted to forge ahead with a style of motorcycle that owed little to the goofy, high-concept machines being flogged endlessly on cable television by the likes of Orange County Choppers and *Build or Bust*. Café racers seem to have, at least momentarily, provided a fresh palette for back street builders, some of whom have grown tired of choppers. Café racers offer deep stylistic rewards with none of the thrills and challenges involved in building or riding a high-performance streetbike.

"I've built dozens of choppers, but to be honest, it's just kind of low on substance. Nobody rides the things because they don't perform and nobody wants to get them dirty. But when you look at an old café racer, the hairs on the back of your neck stand up wondering what it was like to actually

Café racer overload in the form of a six-cylinder Honda CBX1000: Doing the ton has never been easier. Simon Green

push one of these homemade things over the ton." That's how award-winning Canadian custom motorcycle wizard, Roger Goldammer, explained his sudden switch from wide-tire, stretch choppers to café racers during the early twenty-first century.

This growing curiosity about the contemporary café racer scene was something I'd experienced myself only a few years earlier. After building and riding my own Triton café racer, I was eager to immerse myself further into the café racer scene as there were few like-minded riders anywhere near my hometown. A trip to the U.K. for the annual Rocker Reunion rally at the Ace Café was a no-brainer, I thought, and soon I was on my way to the British Isles. As with most travel, the best

A German custom version of Kawasaki's W650, a cult motorcycle based on the original Kawasaki W1 of the late 1960s. Simon Green

experiences are typically those that are completely unplanned and unexpected. During my first visit to the Rocker Reunion rally, I'd made a point of arriving on a Friday when I could catch the weekly gathering of motorcycles on the Chelsea Bridge in west London. The well-lighted bridge, built in 1937,had been attracting hundreds and sometimes thousands of motorcyclists for decades and, having made a brief pass through a happy, throttle-wringing mob of bikes a few years earlier, I was eager to return.

Taking the tube from Victoria Station one stop to Sloane Square, I ended up walking the last few blocks to the bridge, which was completely deserted in the early evening sunset. Walking farther along, I spotted a quaint, empty pub and settled inside to wait for the Chelsea Bridge crowd while enjoying a few pints. After a few moments the elderly barman, dressed from Central Casting in a bow tie and black apron, approached, carefully eyeing my black leather jacket the whole time. "Excuse me, but are you a rocker, by chance?" he asked curiously. "Because if you are," he continued before I could answer, "there's a right good rocker pub just down the road with rock-and-roll and motorbikes."

Sure enough, just around the corner stood the Pavilion pub, its sidewalk covered in café racers and the sound of vintage rockabilly throbbing from the open door. Inside, it was as if I'd stepped into a weird wrinkle in the space-time continuum; the stage held a quartet of aging musicians dressed in early 1960s sharkskin suits, while a phalanx of men in black leather jackets, engineer boots, jeans, and greasy hair twirled their tarted-up female dates around in a wild, swing-dance. I knew not a soul inside the Pavilion that night, but by asking a couple of questions about the café racers parked at the curb, I made a few friends for life.

Rocker Cecil Taylor (foreground) was part of the multiethnic crowd at the Ace Café during the ton-up days. "Nobody cared what color you were as long as you were fast on a motorbike." Author's collection

The nightly crowds at the Ace a good half century in the past. They came searching for speed, for friends and a place to call their own, just like today. Author's collection

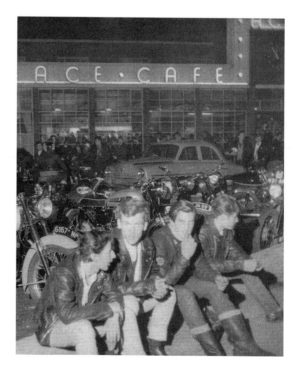

The pub, I learned, hadn't changed a bit since it started hosting rock-and-roll music back in the early 1960s. The nearby neighborhood of Battersea just across the river had been a rocker stronghold back then, I learned from Rocker Bill, a tall, wiry café racer whose jacket was covered in Johnny Kidd and the Pirates logos. In 1968, when a young movie director named Ken Loach filmed the socially charged drama *Up the Junction* here in 1968, the Pavilion and several of its resident rockers (many of whom were present that night) worked as on-camera extras, while the house band, the Flames, are rumored to have opened for the Beatles, Carl Perkins, and other bands of note.

Much has been written about the very British concept of mate-ship that is said to have been the glue binding rockers to each other. Such closeness existed between the crowds at the Pavilion that I felt at times as if I'd inadvertently wandered into a small family reunion. Many of the riders had owned their café racers since at least the 1970s, and such long-term ownership made for men who were familiar with every nut and bolt on their machines along with an encyclopedic knowledge of what made them faster. Many boasted of knowing Father Bill Shergold of the 59 Club personally and of being

Italian rider Giuseppe Brigante on his hand-built Motobi café racer. Stand in the café forecourt long enough, and every fast motorcycle ever made will roll past. Simon Green

French rocker aboard one of Voxan's brilliant Black Magic factory custom café racers—the 998cc V-twin competed in the 2005 Isle of Man TT Production race where it accounted for itself well in a field dominated by Japanese superbikes. Simon Green

Milwaukee's Fuel Café, America's café racer headquarters in the Midwest. Author's collection

"persuaded" by teachers, judges, and parents to join the group as a means of keeping out of trouble.

Thick were the tales about "embarrassing some young git on their GSX-whatever on the local roundabout" and, with the fury these guys exhibited entering and leaving the Pavilion, I'd have to take some of these tales as truth. It was a heady, wonderful experience, and it was difficult to tear myself away

and head back over to the Chelsea Bridge where I'd hoped to photograph some of the motorcycles.

By the time I arrived back at the bridge, darkness had descended and the high-pitched whines and roars of modern sportbikes were thick in the air. Dozens of brightly colored machines had lined both inside lanes of the span, and a tiny chip stall was serving that wonderfully artery-clogging fare common in British life, fish and chips. Strange thing was, after relating my tale of serendipitously finding a genuine rocker pub to a few sportbike riders, the crowd mostly shrugged indifferently. It seems the café racer movement may have planted the technological seeds for the Speed Triples and Suzuki Bandits these motorcyclists rode, but few of these modern riders had any clue about, or interest in, their country's motorcycling heritage.

A while later, one of the rockers from the Pavilion turned up on his Norton model 600, a beautifully appointed classic street racer that sparkled under the glow of the streetlamps. I seemed to be the only person present, besides the old-timer in the chip stall, who appreciated the motorcycle.

By the time I returned to the Rocker reunion a few years later, there were more modern sportbike riders in attendance, and the sight of Yamaha R1s and Honda CBRs is a far more common sight along the Brighton Promenade than it once was. For café racer fans who've always wondered what it's like to see the real thing in action, for serious café racer heads, a visit to the Ace during Rocker Reunion week is like Christmas, a Moto GP round, and working as an extra on *The Leatherboys* all rolled into one—well, without the rocker flick's homoerotic overtones. Instead, what you get is not a hokey shrine to Britain's past, but a lively transport café where truckers, local office workers, and, yes, plenty of bikers congregate for stick-to-your ribs chow, warm pints, and a bit of history.

"The Americans have the whole Harley-Davidson thing with Sturgis and the Rock Store, but I've always viewed the rocker period as something uniquely British that was worth preserving," said Ace Café owner Wilsmore, a dedicated biker who once worked as a horseback-mounted police constable in London.

There may be plenty of original greasers parked up here, but the scene at the Ace on a Friday before a big event reveals just how many riders are eager to create café bikes out of modern machinery. In one small pack came the German W650 Club, mostly middle-aged oddballs who saw an instant classic in Kawasaki's stunning-but-unpopular retro parallel twin. Some had built period-perfect café racer replicas from their Kawas, hand-pounding aluminum gas tanks, installing tiny bum-stop seats,

and machining rear-sets in home workshops.

Giuseppe Briganti, a police helicopter pilot from Pesaro, Italy, rode across the Alps, through Spain, and ferried his rare, 1971 Motobi Tornado to England, "just to ride with the rockers. At home, they are all Ducati, all the time. Here, I feel like one of the guys and am able to speak about the motorcycles that I love." With his stiletto boots, vintage leathers, and pompadour, Briganti was 100 percent rocker. He was proud of his country's class-leading motorcycles and most of his friends back home were better versed in Aprilia than BSA, but Brigante's dedication to early speed was typical of this crowd, regardless of their country of origin.

"There are many fine bikes to ride in Italy, but I decided to choose with my heart and picked this Motobi because it is an Italian version of a classic

Ton-up vicars: Father Bill Shergold (left) shepherded the 59 Club's Classics Section for a half century with the assistance of the Rev. Graham Hulett. Author's collection

Café racers are a common sight in the Big Apple thanks to Scotsman Hugh Mackie's efforts.(far right) Author's collection

Opposite page: Rockers gathering for one of the frequent charity rides organized by the 59 Club as a means of dispelling the negative press associated at motorcyclists. The tradition lives on today. Author's collection

rocker's machine," he explained with the requisite Mediterranean hand gestures.

Briganti rode 300 kilometers on this journey, most of it at speeds near the ton on a motorcycle that was in production for so few years, replacement parts are scarcer than ape-hangers on a Triton. Outfitted with then industry-leading components like a four-leading shoe Grimeca drum brake, electric starting, and roadracing-style Marzocchi

forks, the Motobi was manufactured by the Benelli motorcycle clan. Possessing the dedication necessary to ride and maintain a motorcycle like this—let alone ride it at the limit—gives Briganti mucho props at the Ace this day.

Arriving at a slower pace but no less impressive was Marta Garcia Alfonso on her 1951 AJS 350 single. The tiny, Spanish-born brunette roared into the Ace, her one-cylinder bike's exhaust popping a steady beat. She quickly stripped out of her leathers, down to a Betty Page pin-up costume consisting of scarcely more cotton than they pack into the tops of aspirin bottles. If there was a male eye in the place still focused on motorcycles at this point, I'd be surprised.

Alfonso, a single mom, admitted to spending most of her free time at the Ace, where she said it was always easy to find a laugh, learn how to maintain her classic bike, or most important, find other café racers to ride with. With vintage

Bumble in Brighton

With their tradition of sensationalized media, mere mention of the words *Brighton* and *fast motorbikes* was once enough to cause panic among the British public. During the early 1960s, when packs of mostly working-class rockers clashed with middle-class mods at seaside resorts like Margate, Blackpool, and Brighton, the press, hungry for headlines, depicted the youthful shenanigans as something akin to the L.A. riots, the battle of Sevastopol, and the Black Plague on two wheels. Closer to the truth, most mods and rockers were from the same schools and neighborhoods. Their legendary pitched battles may have sold newspapers, but violence was rare.

"I was here, at Brighton back in '65, and we didn't rumble, we just drank too many pints," laughed Bob Gibson of Slough, England. Like several thousand attendees at recent Rocker reunions, Gibson, fifty-eight, rode a customized scooter, not a café racer. "The papers said it was all shock-horror, but back in the '60s, my Lambretta broke down and a group of rockers stopped and repaired it for me. We were mostly friends then and we're still friends now."

Gibson's opposite number from back in the day, Dan Stuart, remembers his days as a café racing rocker not for violence but the glory of empty roads, cheap petrol, and pretty girls. "What was Brighton like back then?" he asked. "For one thing, it wasn't half this crowded. All these chaps claiming to have been rockers, most of 'em weren't even born in '65."

Stuart, who at sixty-nine still gets around on a Triumph Sprint ST, says so many contemporary riders are attracted to the period because it represents a more innocent time for motorcyclists. "There were none of these bloody speed cameras clicking your photo and mailing you a ticket. There were nights when we'd go for a burn-up from the Busy Bee [café] down to the Ace, out to Squires [café], and then do the whole circuit again. Cars had only three gears so we could outrun anything. I think that's what these young lads missed out on."

One tragic element of the time-honored burn-ups on crowded public roads has not changed much over the years, unfortunately. While heading toward the Brighton seafront, traffic, already stop-and-go for much of the 68-mile trek from London, ground to a halt a few miles north of our destination. Rounding a bend cordoned off with orange traffic cones, I spotted the body of Marta Garcia Alfonso lying in the road, lifeless after a collision with a car that had stopped abruptly in front of her AJS. A moment of silence was observed in her honor along the Brighton seafront, and graying rockabillies ceased swing dancing long enough to honor the dead rider. As kick-start levers were pounced upon for the rides back home, the death of a rider put this event and the café racer revival into stark perspective. As I'd heard again and again during my visit, "Anybody can ride a new fast bike, but it takes guts to ride an old motorbike fast."

rockabilly blaring from the house sound-system, a parking lot full of shiny, exotic bikes, and pin-up models prancing around, the effect was almost surreal. It was like a café racer theme park, replete with gift shop and checkered-flag wallpaper.

But there had to be more to this scene than just standing around admiring each other's gear. What I came for was a genuine burn-up with the rockers, a high-speed tangle with Stonebridge Park's famously homicidal traffic. Finding a crew willing to fulfill this wish wasn't tough. Borrowing Wilsmore's Triumph Speed Triple 1050—a machine carrying at least the elementary DNA of classic café racers—a quartet of us wheeled out of the Ace and roared through the red brick underpasses, one emblazoned with an ominous ad for Ferodo brake pads that has reminded riders to check their stoppers for half a century. Brakes would play heavily into the next few minutes as the other riders began diving between tiny, almost invisible gaps in traffic and stretching their throttle cables, even as rush-hour traffic thickened.

This was the stretch of road where the rockers proved themselves, first dodging the cars launched out of the blind side street Beresford Avenue, and then running a high-speed loop on the North Circular that would inevitably position the motorcycles for a full 100-mile-per-hour pass in front of the Ace.

This route is fraught with potential mishaps, though. Despite the horrendous traffic, London's transport minister's staff imagine theirs to be a pedestrian-friendly town, so most sidewalks are surrounded by waist-high, steel railings, the rungs about 6 inches apart. Whizzing by these human cheese-graters at considerable velocity on a capable, modern Speed Triple was hairy enough. That a generation of British riders prided themselves on doing so aboard homemade café racers with weak, drum brakes is chill-inducing stuff. This also explains the legends, urban and otherwise, I heard of rockers who failed to negotiate corners and ended up on the other side of these railings looking like black leather Spam cans.

Rocker legend and Triton expert Dave Degens was a regular on these same roads during the 1950s and explained how quickly things could switch from thrilling to heart stopping. "I can remember one time when a group of us went away from the Ace and two or three of the Herberts [police] followed us out because we were on quite nice bikes. They were following us 'round, but I was quite quick because I had started racing at that time. There was a left-hand bend, and I could get round it quite quick, about 90 to 100 miles per hour; I did this and as I turned around, somebody had gone into the wire fence," he said.

Bob Gibson of Slough, England is a regular at the Rocker Reunion events despite favoring Vespa to Triton. Gibson, a veteran of the 1960s, says the mods versus rockers enmity was largely overblown. Simon Green

Rocker Cecil Richards recalled a time when the assumed risks of riding fast on this section of dual carriageway were more than worth it for the friendship and closeness of the café racer scene: "When I first went to the Ace with a guy I knew from school and his friends, they explained to me where it was and off we went. As soon as we were on the North Circular they went berserk and I was plodding along on my little bike. I remember when I saw the Ace Café, I gave a hand signal and drove into the Ace to the biggest applause you've ever heard in your life, everyone was clapping, and I just didn't know what to do with myself.

"In 1961, I was the first black man ever to go to the Ace as a biker. So everyone welcomed me and brought me a coffee and a bun. We sat down and began talking, and one of the first things one of them said to me was, 'When are you going to

No time for ambivalence, this 1960s rocker wants everyone to know who he is, despite the additional police scrutiny such labels could bring. Author's collection

blame the peer-enforced code of riding like a true rocker with your throttle to the stop as often as possible. Whatever the case, by the time I returned to the Ace Café, everyone else was inside, ordering tea. After a ride like this, you nearly shudder to imagine what it must have been like in a real burn-up, on dark, damp streets.

This strange, almost religious dedication to speed affects rockers, new and old, I'd come to learn. It's not enough to simply wear the gear and own the café racer. "Part of the attraction, part of the strong draw of attending a rally like this is finding those rare individuals who share a passion for the same kind of motorbikes," explained Martine Spesser. "Anybody can go out and purchase a fast, brand new motorbike like a GSX-R, but to ride an original café racer fast, that takes practice and dedication." Spesser rode in with representatives of the French 59 Club, a church charity created to deflect bad publicity and lend sanctuary to youthful rockers in the

get a bike?' I said, 'I've got a bike.' He said, 'That's not a bike, that's a peashooter!' I ended up going seven days a week. It was the most welcoming and happy place that I've ever been."

During my high-speed run from the Ace, the Speed Triple may have had a thirty-five-year, 75-horsepower advantage over the leaky Norton Atlases and BSA Lightnings riding in our group, but keeping up with them proved a lost cause. Blame riding on the wrong side of the road, blame the fact that I'd like to live to see middle age, or

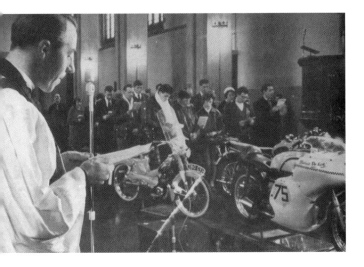

Father Bill Shergold conducts one of his famous "Ton-Up Services" in an effort to embrace the often-scorned rockers. His efforts paid off with thousands joining the 59 Club under his direction. Author's collection

A newspaper editorial cartoon poking fun at Shergold's efforts captured the generation gap between the ton-up kids and their parents. Author's collection

THIS IS A
PERSONAL INVITATION
TO
YOU
TO COME TO CHURCH NEXT SUNDAY
MAY 13TH. AT 3 PM. FOR A

SPECIAL SERVICE
FOR
MOTOR CYCLISTS

BE HELD AT THE ETON MISSION, EASTWAY.
HACKNEY WICK E.9.

TERWARDS YOU ARE WELCOME TO COME AND ENJOY
URSELF IN THE 59 CLUB'S COFFEE BAR.

YOU AREN'T SURE HOW TO GET TO HACKNEY WICK RING
AMH 5475 AND ASK FOR FATHER SHERGOLD—
O WILL GLADLY GIVE YOU DIRECTIONS.

early 1960s. The club has become a hallowed part of the café racer scene, its black-and-white shoulder patch signifying true credentials.

For Spesser, joined by her husband, Claude, and a dozen followers on a slew of bitchin' Voxan retros, making the run from London to Brighton is part religious Haaj and part summer vacation. "We fell in love with things from the 1960s, the rock-and-roll and the bikes, mostly," she said. "We come to the Ace Café three or four times each year to remember where fast motorbikes came from. It's very important."

4

Café'd Production Bikes

Café as both a verb and adverb! "Café'd" is a shortened form of "café racer-ized," i.e., a motorcycle that has been modified in the café-racer style.

Motorcycle enthusiasts are a fickle bunch. Often, in the letters pages of enthusiast publications, riders will complain about the way manufacturers ignore their input when it comes to designing new motorcycles. The factories give us air-cooled twins and we scream for in-line fours; for every multipurpose machine rolling out of a showroom, there's a disgruntled rider wishing to see more supersports machines on the market. And when manufacturers do acknowledge what custom builders are doing by offering factory customs, retros, and concept

Page 96: *Steve Carpenter still doing it the old-fashioned way, scouring junkyards for unwanted motorcycles and creating testaments to speed from their remains. Carpy's collection includes a Rickman Honda as well as several British classics.* Aaron Hollebecke

bikes, seldom does the motorcycling public embrace their efforts.

A prime example of a factory custom that failed to find an audience was Honda's handsome GB500 single of the late 1980s. A classically styled tribute to the café'd CB450s that raced on circuits and public roads forty years earlier, the GB, with its squared gas tank, dropped bars, and period-perfect rubber fork gaiters looked like the motorcycle anyone considering a café racer would have wanted at the time. Sure, the 500's single-cylinder, four-valve motor was not going to take home many checkered flags in the Stoplight

This 1970s Yamaha XS650-based café racer may not be constructed from a genuine Rickman Metisse chassis, it still reflects an admirable job of creating a classic speedster from relatively new bits; fiberglass Manx replica gas tank and home-brewed seat are a triumph. Auth or's collection

Grand Prix with just 33 horses pulsing through the narrow, 18-inch rear tire, but sales were so poor that Honda dropped the machine—and apparently, any subsequent plans to reinvest in the retro market—in the United States after just two years and 4,500 units sold.

Thankfully, not all attempts to design factory motorcycles that appeal to café racers have met such tepid responses: The motorcycles featured here were all created by engineers and designers who were aware of the public's cravings for speed and style. The early models, such as Velocette's Venom Thruxton and Triumph's Bonneville, were yesterday's versions of today's superbikes. They provided speed-hungry riders with what were basically street-legal versions of the motorcycles they'd watched their track-going heroes ride to great acclaim.

Like today's superbikes, these café'd production machines could be a handful for beginners to operate, and their cost sometimes defied the limits of customer common sense and good judgment. But the visceral appeal of a motorcycle that appeared to have just rolled in from a pit lane was, and is, irresistible to many riders.

A production café racer may have seemed like heresy to purists who believe a true café racer is always a DIY project, a machine that should be as unique in its approach to performance as the person designing it. But in all honesty, not everyone with an eye for doing tons was a gifted motorcycle technician. There were pitfalls by the score awaiting novice builders, and it was not hard to try and modify a perfectly fine stock motorcycle into a café racer and end up with something far worse than either. The production café racers serve this segment of the audience well, while providing some beautiful templates from which more talented mechanics could improve.

It should come as no surprise that Britain's motorcycle manufacturers mined the specials and customs they spotted on the streets, in race meet parking lots, and at industry shows for their own ideas. The café racers emerging from countless

small garages and one-man assembly lines were often amazing for their ingenuity, style, and ability to wring that last ounce of performance from an engine. There was little chance that the factories, struggling to compete, at first with each other and later, with the Japanese, would ignore concepts like the graceful, nickel-plated Rickman Metisse café racer frames that propelled riders to victory on racetracks. Triumph, after all, conceded, having

Launched in 1978, Suzuki's GS1000 was the Hamamatsu firm's response to the café racer aftermarket. This machine's brutal acceleration was undermined by its mediocre chassis. Author's collection

Yamaha, like Honda, made its mark racing on the Isle of Man, allowing their race-bred motorcycles to take a mild café racer flavor in showroom form; this 1965 YDS3C 250 two-stroke proved mildly popular with British café racers. Author's collection

Beautiful and bold, Ducati's bevel-drive desmo twin 750 Sport of 1972 was—and remains—one of the most desirable factory café racers ever devised. Author's collection

been bested at the chassis game and hired on the Rickman Brothers to design its factory racebike frames.

The work of visionary café racer tuners like chassis designer Colin Seeley or Triton building expert Ian Kennedy no doubt played a role in the creation of late-model British streetbikes such as the Norton Commando and Triumph Trident, the latter graced with lines that were clearly inspired by specials. It's a symbiotic relationship that continues to this day, as factories observe,

and eventually absorb the scene from the streets, ultimately selling it back to the public in a repackaged form.

In more recent years, the trend continues as production café racers aimed at the nostalgia market grow in both number and popularity. There are still chicken-and-egg debates about who built the first true retro café racer, and it is a bit strange to view Baines Racing's stunning Ducati 900ss retro kit next to a Ducati Sport Classic which, coincidentally, arrived four years behind John and Jeff Baines's strikingly similar, home-brewed version (which the pair say was first sketched out on a cigarette pack in a pub!). But nothing was engineered in a vacuum, the old saying goes, proven to a point by the production café racers.

Prompting a worldwide resurgence in factory café racers was the 2006 line of Ducati Sport Classics. The GT shares the dual-spark 1000cc motor with Ducati's Multistrada, made even more sexy by Michigan's BellaCorse. Mike Selman

This Aermacchi Chimera café racer bears the design hallmarks of a motorcycle conceived during a period of stylistic experimentation— the middle 1950s. Odd, but nice and clearly some inspiration for Ariel and its Leader. Author's collection

A pristine Royal Enfield 750cc Interceptor from 1967 in the Barber Motorsports Museum in Alabama displays the height of factory café accessorizing during the late ton-up era. Author's collection

A stunning example of a Norton Commando given a Domiracer treatment; bikini fairing is Ducati Monster-like while drilled primary cover reveals a Hayward belt drive primary. Author's collection

A modern café racer for the masses: Ducati's Monster. Note the distinctive and very effective steel trellis frame that made naked sport motorcycles popular again. This one is the S4 range topper. Simon Green

Minnesota Harley-Davidson technician Greg "Softail Doc" Hageman has made some impressive café racers from Yamaha's venerable XS650 twin, including this fully faired, Dunstall look-alike. Greg Hageman

Brilliant remake of the modern Bonneville from Sel-Moto, featuring a gas tank borrowed from a Honda CB750F Supersport mated to a tuned Bonneville engine and a tail section of the owner's design. Mike Selman

Honda's first attempt at marketing a retro café racer in the form of the 1989 GB500 sold sparsely, but has since become a cult classic. Author's collection

Benelli's excellent, 1130ss three-cylinder Café Racer exhibiting its high-speed cornering agility by Joe Tatora of Supermoto Italia. Simon Green

Bologna, Italy's Moto Morini provided Europeans with one of the finest factory café racers in the nimble little 3-1/2 Sport (or 3.5) of the mid-1970s; the zippy, mid sized street racer looked good, cornered admirably, and ran like a true thoroughbred. Bauer Media

Another timeless take on the café racer theme by Greg Hageman utilizing a Yamaha XS650 engine and a host of hand-made and early Yamaha parts including a late 1960s XS fuel cell, Airtech racing seat, and vintage Yamaha drum brakes. Greg Hageman

A veritable crazy quilt of hand-bent exhaust headers, one-off fiberglass café bodywork, and lustrous red paint are not what you'd expect to see on an original café racer, but this Honda CB750 roadster turns heads nevertheless. Aaron Hollebecke

Red, quick, and capable of cornering with stiletto-like sharpness, Ducati's Sport 1000 makes the most of its dual-spark 1,000cc desmodue engine. Ducati Motor Holdings S.p.A.

No Speed Like Old Speed

Walk into any modern motorcycle showroom and punters will face an intimidating choice of dozens of different motorcycles from equally as many genres and subgenres. What most of them share are truly modern levels of performance, with even the lowliest four-stroke scooter offering superior acceleration and braking prowess, not to mention reliability, over a vintage motorcycle. But the plug-and-go capabilities of modern sporting tackle is part of the reason why the vintage café racer maintains a hallowed position among serious speed merchants. Why, exactly? Well, most aficionados will attest to enjoying the challenge of riding a motorcycle lacking radial disc brake calipers, race-derived radial tires, and a power-to-weight ratio that would shame an F-20 fighter jet.

Anybody can ride a new motorcycle fast, but it takes real skill and big balls to ride an old motorcycle fast. That's a café racer's mantra I've heard repeated everywhere from the Cat and Fiddle Pass to California's Laguna Seca Raceway.

Hang around any vintage race meet or café racer gathering and you'll notice an immense pride among riders who've shown a rear tire to some sportbike pilot riding a more modern piece of machinery. This at least partly explains the endless tuning sessions and the remarkable intimacy with which a veteran café racer will know his or her machine; the thriving vintage Britbike aftermarket that keeps these machines alive (see appendix) ensures a skilled rider on a Matchless G50 can make a fool of a less experienced rider aboard this year's hottest Suzuki GSX-R. In fact, the only American Isle of Man TT champion, New Yorker Dave Roper, set a lap record aboard just such a machine in the 1984 Tourist Trophy event, setting a lap time of 120 miles per hour, on a vintage Matchless café racer boasting only 48 rear-wheel horsepower.

It would be several years before an American rider aboard a fully modern racebike could match Roper's blistering pace, which he set aboard a motorcycle plagued with mechanical problems, so the story goes, that an exhaust-header bolt was swallowed by the gaping bellmouth on the Matchless single's Amal carburetor, only to come rattling out of the exhaust pipe a few miles later!

Dave Roper, the last and to date, only American to win an Isle of Man Tourist Trophy race, accomplishing the feat in 1984 on a Team Obsolete Matchless G50. Author's collection

One of my favorite illustrations of the ability of vintage café racers to compete with modern motorcycles came to light with a story featuring the famously cantankerous, seven-time Grand Prix champ Phil Read. The story was featured in 1998 in Britain's always marvelous *Classic Bike* magazine in which Read decried the flash and unnecessary risk of the modern knee-down generation as evidence that modern speed merchants had lost the plot. To further his point, Read challenged editor Mark Forsyth to a few laps around the 1.48-mile Cadwell Park roadrace circuit with one rather bally stipulation: Read would lap the track on his 55-horsepower Molnar Manx Norton while Forsyth would be given carte blanche to navigate Cadwell on a 1998 Yamaha R11. Read wasn't taking leave of his senses. Rather, he was determined to prove that for most street riding and even many track circumstances, the 50-odd horsepower generated by a classic café

Roper in action vaulting the 500cc Matchless single over the hump at Balaugh Bridge. The Matchless, we are told, swallowed one of its own carburetor bolts during the race which came bounding out of the open megaphone exhaust! Author's collection

racer was more than enough for most riders.

True to his point, Read lapped the circuit just at a best time of 1 minute 22.60 seconds, which proved less than 2 seconds slower than the magazine editor (best lap time 1 minute 21.47 seconds) on a motorcycle producing nearly three times as much horsepower. Read, riding in the bolt-upright, knees-against-the-petrol-tank style popular during the café racer era, even used his right foot to help create back pressure for his bellowing open megaphone exhaust when accelerating up one of the circuit's towering hills, proving that, in the right hands, the old machines can still represent themselves nicely.

1964 Triumph Bonneville Thruxton

Engine: Air-cooled, two-valve, OHV parallel twin
Displacement: 649cc
Power: 47 brake horsepower
Weight: 395 pounds
Top speed: 110 miles per hour

1964 TRIUMPH BONNEVILLE THRUXTON

Triumph may own the name perhaps most closely aligned with British motorcycling during the 1960s, but the Meriden firm was most reluctant to enter the factory café racer field alongside its marketplace competitors. Triumph, after all, enjoyed a respected standing in the motorcycle market similar to that of Honda today. As a sales leader with decades of prestige and dedicated customer brand loyalty to its credit—and some 250,000 Bonnevilles sold worldwide during their production run—playing to the street-racing crowd wasn't in Triumph's best interests.

Still, the win-on-Sunday sell-on-Monday ethos was unavoidable when it came to placing feet on showroom floors. Honda eventually joined the production café racer fray in 1965 when it offered a limited-edition version of the unit construction T120 Bonnie in Thruxton trim. Named in honor of the British short circuit where the 650cc Bonneville would enjoy many racing victories, both as a scratcher and endurance

racer, the Thruxton was a tour de force of factory performance upgrades, delivered, naturally, at a very high-performance price.

For 365 pounds (or 65 pounds dearer than a standard Bonneville), the Thruxton offered riders the status of beefier racing forks, dropped handlebars, a steeper 25-degree rake, a humpbacked racing seat, and a tuned version of the proven, reliable (and very vibey) 649cc parallel twin engine churning out 48 brake horsepower. The Thruxton could reach 125 miles per hour in fourth gear in street trim, and close to 130 with an aftermarket fairing clamped on for extra aerodynamics. If there was a weak link it was the double-leading shore front brakes that were mercifully replaced by disc models in 1968, just before the Bonneville grew in displacement to 750cc with the introduction of the oil-in-frame model of 1972.

Only fifty-eight factory Thruxtons were ever built, but the die was nevertheless cast. Triumph offered the faster machine's performance upgrades to Bonneville owners everywhere and a legend was subsequently born. With head porting, lump camshafts, and big-bore carburetors, the owner of a "normal" Bonneville T120 could approach the Thruxton's hallowed performance figures and many surpassed those figures.

1977 DUCATI 900SS

During the café racer era, Ducatis were not renowned as the class-leading superbikes they are today. However, their 350cc bevel-drive singles, characterized by the firm's unique, Desmodronic valve-actuation system, were beautiful, nimble roadsters of the first order. It wasn't until engineers at the Bologna, Italy, manufacturer experimented with a new, sand-cast crankcase that allowed the mounting of two 350cc cylinders together did the company's reputation for unsurpassed performance and graceful styling come into its own.

In 1972, British racer Paul Smart piloted a 750cc version of this thoroughbred machine to victory in the prestigious Imola 200 road race, permanently cementing the big Ducati's place in motorcycling history; and after the success of the 750GT and 750 Sport in the mid-1970s, Ducati upped its game by boring out the engine to

1977 Ducati 900 SS

Engine: Air-cooled, two-valve, desmodronic 90-degree twin
Displacement: 864cc
Power: 79 brake horsepower
Weight 444 pounds
Top speed: 130 miles per hour

The Terrible Tiddlers:
Small Displacement Café Racers

Though names like Bonneville, Triton, and Rocket Gold Star are clearly recognized as the heavy-hitters of the café racer scene; in reality, many less illustrious machines were ridden during the time, often in greater numbers than the better-known motorcycles. Money was always scarce for youthful motorcyclists in those days and maintaining the employment or, more important, the credit to purchase a big-bore streetbike could stretch the resources of many. By 1961, the British government had placed a 250cc limit on new riders' motorbikes, furthering the need for learner bikes. No problem, the motorcycle manufacturers replied, serving up a broad roster of small-displacement machines aimed at novices and those not seeking the thrills and responsibilities of riding higher-end motorcycles.

Among the most distinctive of these baby café racers, and due to its strange looks, one of the most polarizing was the Ariel Leader. With its dainty lines and bright, two-tone paint draped across a fully enclosed body that could shame a Helix scooter, Ariel's 250cc two-stroke Leader nevertheless found favor with many budget-minded café racers. The Leader, which could have been mistaken for a prop from an Audrey Hepburn comedy, boasted an 18-horsepower twin-cylinder engine that propelled it and rider to a respectable 70 miles per hour. While its tiny drum brakes were considered among the worst going and the sight of its strange trailing axle front end still causes outbreaks of rampant head-scratching, the Ariel Leader was the little motorcycle that café racers loved to hate. Because it sold fairly well, Ariel came upon the idea of removing the controversial bodywork and re-introducing the machine to the market as the Ariel Arrow, which, with 22 horsepower, could at least keep up with the tail end of a pack of "proper" motorcycles.

BSA provided access to the world of performance riding with its Bantam model, a spritely little streetbike offered in 125, 150, and 175cc versions. Ridden by British Royal Mail telegram delivery men, this, too, was an odd-looking machine, known for its dual, vertically mounted springs on the sprung rear wheel hub, the Bantam's tiny engine looked lonely sitting in the massive engine bay. Still, riders on the small end of the age scale loved the Bantam, which could hit 65 miles per hour and hold there for miles. At a mere 150 pounds, the little Bantams were fun to whip around a series of bands, and tales abound of small-bike riders passing some well-known faster café racers

BSA's four-stroke single may have been overshadowed in the performance wars by larger, faster machines but was nonetheless quick enough in a narrow, winding road. Bauer Media

Who needs big bore motorcycles when Royal Enfield's 250cc Crusader Clubman looked the business and offered scintillating performance? The little factory custom came equipped with dropped bars and a 8.5:1 compression engine good for 80 miles per hour and 90 miles per gallon. This model sports an aftermarket bikini fairing with front numberplate displayed horizontally. Bauer Media

in the right set of corners. As these younger riders grew a few years older and a few pounds wealthier, many moved up to BSA's C12 and C15 Starfire, a 250cc four-stroke single with impressive performance for its size.

There was an inherent inferiority complex among riders aboard these types of motorcycles, and as a result, many thrashed their machines mercilessly in an effort to keep up with bigger bikes. Thankfully, in these days of roadside top-end repairs, pushrod-operated valves, and air-cooling fins, repairing a worn-out tiddler was not only easy, it provided valuable mechanical experience.

Despite how little has been written about the smaller cafés, the fact that an aftermarket was built around them proves their popularity. BSA's Starfire, for example, could be outfitted with high-lift cams, high-compression 10.5:1 pistons, and all the café racer essentials from fiberglass fuel tanks and open bellmouths for the tiny, small-bore Amal carb. In this state of tune, a rider could expect to see 85 miles per hour with a strong tailwind, which must have been quite a rush for a motorcycle barely larger than a Vespa scooter.

Few tiddlers were as well-known and ubiquitous as Triumph's Tiger Cub, a hard-running little 250cc four-stroke single available

by 1961 in a beefier (relatively) Sports Cub version. Both models were known affectionately as "The Baby Bonnie" for its miniature Bonneville-look gas tank, forks, and seat. For a small-displacement bike, the folks at triumph spared little detail in kitting out the Cub, including an energy-transfer ignition, a 376 Amal monobloc carburetor with remote float bowl, 9 to 1 compression ratio pegs, and a high-performance "R" or racing camshaft. Top speed was somewhere in the neighborhood of 85 miles per hour. Like the bigger Triumphs, the Cub could be tuned endlessly, though most owners longed, more than anything, for upgraded brakes as the beer-mat sized stoppers attached to the Cub's front end were the stuff of nightmares.

Perhaps the best-looking of the small-bore café racers was made by Royal Enfield, whose racy Continental GT was a sales hit from the start. With its long, narrow fiberglass gas tank, tiny windscreen, and café racer accessories from stock, the machine's 1964 reveal at the London Motorcycle Show was a jaw-dropper. Enfield had sold a solid, if not earth-shaking, number of its 750 Interceptor twin since 1962, but the Continental GT, designed with assistance from the company's youngest employees, made the Interceptor look like something Grandpa would ride. Clutching the low Clubman handlebars and twisting the throttle, the little Enfield would eventually thump its merry way to 85 miles per hour. This machine, too, spawned something of a tuning cottage industry during the mid-1960s, where owners could buy the usual performance upgrade products.

This motorcycle's styling was so well-executed that when the Royal Enfield Company of India (where production continued after ceasing in the U.K. in 1968) decided to produce a newfangled café racer, it simply bolted its 450cc four-stroke single into a slightly updated Continental GT chassis.

Great-looking as it was, there were problems. The GT's five-speed transmission was said to be as fragile as a teenage ego, and Triumph's Cub, despite being less hip in the looks department, would show it a clean set of tires. Despite its good looks, Continental owners had their hands full when it came to keeping their machines in running condition.

86x74.4 millimeters to produce the legendary 900 Super Sport. Cradled by a unique and somewhat fragile-looking tubular steel frame and dressed in a sexy blue and silvery livery with long, chromed megaphone exhausts, the 900SS was one of the most stunning factory café racers ever built.

With its distinctive 90-degree L-twin engine configuration, curvaceous bikini fairing, massively effective Brembo disc brakes, and top-class Marzocchi suspension, the SS handled better than just about any other motorcycle during the early 1970s. The Desmo twin pumped out massive quantities of torque from around 3,000 rpm and throughout the meaty midrange. Overall power output was an impressive 79 brake horsepower, which catapulted the SS to a 130-mile-per-hour top speed. If there's one downside to this classic café racer it's that, being a small concern, Ducati produced only a few hundred SS models per year in those days, which has subsequently driven the price of a genuine SS model into a realm available only to the very wealthy.

1959 BSA GOLD STAR CLUBMAN

Easily the most famous single-cylinder motorcycle in history, the BSA Gold Star, whether in 350cc or 500cc form, represented a watershed in production performance motorcycles. The design's simplicity—the single, 85x88-millimeter cylinder pounded out its distinctive cadence in a lightweight all-aluminum cylinder, which was revolutionary when introduced to a speed-thirsty market as a 350 in 1938. By the 1950s, BSA—which had manufactured weapons during World War II as Birmingham Small Arms Company—had perfected its brew, adding the Goldie's trademark curved, flat seat, swept-back exhaust (which would be copied endlessly by both the café racer aftermarket and other manufacturers) and chromed gas tank side panels. Later versions really played up the whole "factory racer" angle and came equipped with a bulbous, 5-gallon endurance racing gas tank, 34-millimeter big bore Amal carb, and close-ratio gearbox for quicker gear-changes.

1959 BSA Gold Star Clubman

Engine: Two-valve, air-cooled, OHV single
Displacement: 499cc
Power: 42 brake horsepower
Weight: 350 pounds
Top speed: 110 miles per hour

The most famous and fastest Gold Star was the 500cc DBD34 model which remained in production, selling several thousand models each year, from the 1950s until 1963. Much has been written and debated about the incredible top speed of this machine, which at 110 miles per hour for a single was rather impressive. The Gold Star's secret was simply tall gearing that allowed the lightweight machine to achieve speeds usually associated with larger-capacity motorcycles. Of course tall gearing and tall sprockets had their drawbacks. The Gold Star was notoriously slow off the line and its tall headstock meant the Goldie's forks were on the longish side, which some say negatively affected the handling. But to its legion of fans, that didn't matter. Style, speed, and the Gold Star's legend were all that did.

2003 ROYAL ENFIELD BULLET CLUBMAN

Aimed at riders on the Indian subcontinent and those in England desiring a retro motorcycling experience closer to the 1960s than, say, riding a Triumph Thunderbird, the Royal Enfield Bullet was a modest success for the Indian-based manufacturer. To broaden its market share, Enfield hired Norman Hyde, a veteran café racer tuner and parts designer who created the Royal Enfield Café Racer.

Looking like a customized street special one would have seen in the Café Rising Sun car park some forty-five years ago, the Hyde-Enfield has nailed the racy lines of the era perfectly. Unfortunately, there are those who say the little 500cc four-stroke singles mimic their 1960s predecessors a bit too faithfully, offering questionable reliability and relatively wheezy performance for a modern retro. Nevertheless, the Enfield line has proven very

2003 Royal Enfield Bullet Clubman

Engine: Air-cooled, two-valve, OHV single
Displacement: 499cc
Power:27brake horsepower
Weight:411 pounds
Top speed: 85 miles per hour

durable, rugged, and easy to maintain due to its air-cooled motor and low-tech ancillaries (the 6-inch drum rear brake, for example, can accept replacement shoes from a number of popular mopeds and scooters) café racer line has now grown to four distinct motorcycles, all propelled along by the same, 27-brake horsepower overhead-valve engine, designed as an upgrade of the original 250cc four-stroke single used in the Enfield Continental GT of a generation before.

The machine does sport its share of modern conveniences, including electric start on most models, solid-state electronic ignition systems, halogen headlamps, a four-speed constant mesh gearbox, and a single, 280-millimeter front disc brake. An upgraded Enfield Clubman Electra is also available, offering an air-gulping 32-millimeter Dell'Orto carburetor, a five-speed transmission, and chromed racing exhaust that's good for a solid 30 horsepower. The real attraction of the Enfield Clubman series is its economy, boasting mile-per-gallon figures of more than 70 in most conditions, which isn't shabby for a lightweight (411 pounds wet) motorcycle that can reach 85 miles per hour on a good day. Better yet, the Clubman looks the business, with its dropped bars, boxy Manx-replica gas tank available in either alloy or fiberglass and a nifty, imitation Gold Star muffler.

1976 MOTO GUZZI LE MANS

Few café racer purists envision a motorcycle adorned with a 500-pound wet weight, shaft drive, and roomy dimensions a typical example of the genre, but Moto Guzzi's robust Le Mans has forged a unique place for itself in the café racer lexicon due to its unique attributes. Launched first in 1967 as the V7, it was powered by a 90-degree engine first used in 1960 in a series of odd, three-wheeled Italian military vehicles known as the 3x3. The V-twin motor proved reliable and powerful enough to tackle Italy's steep inclines and, as a result, was soon powering Guzzi's large-displacement road bikes.

The V7 was replaced by the V7 Sport in 1972 in 750cc form, and in 1976, it was rechristened Le Mans, which was clearly aimed at capitalizing on Moto Guzzi's racing heritage, which, by the 1970s was then decades in the past. But the Italian firm clearly knew how to design a nicely balanced sportbike, designing a new, steel trellis frame (with revolutionary, removable lower rails for easy engine removal) for the 844cc horizontally

opposed V-twin. Graced with a long wheelbase that aided stability in corners, the Le Mans was again upgraded with improved 35-millimeter Marzocchi forks and twin rear shocks, as well as new cast-alloy wheels in 1976. The Le Man's pumped out a respectable 72 horsepower from its two-valve heads and took advantage of a five-speed, close-ratio gearbox that propelled it to an impressive rate of speed.

The drilled dual front disc brakes were linked by a servo that activated both front and rear simultaneously and were considered state of the art on a production machine in 1976. They provided abrupt stopping power most rockers would have traded their record collections for only a decade earlier! Two 36-millimeter Dell'Orto carburetors were deployed racing style without any filtration whatsoever, which only adds to this machine's raw, manly appeal.

1976 Moto Guzzi Le Mans

Engine: Air-cooled, two-valve, transverse V-twin
Displacement: 850cc
Power: 72 brake horsepower
Weight: 480 pounds
Top speed: 124 miles per hour

1973 Read Titan Honda

Engine: Air-cooled, two-valve,
    transverse SOHC four
Displacement: 844cc
Power: 71 brake horsepower
Weight: 460 pounds
Top speed: 135 miles per hour

1973 READ TITAN HONDA 750

Stubbornly dedicated to the cause of preserving and promoting British-based specials, few aftermarket houses were quick to jump aboard the Japanese specials bandwagon during the early 1970s. Leytonstone, north London's Read Titan, however, clearly saw the rising sun on the horizon, and began offering up complete café racer kits for popular Japanese machines, including Kawasaki's fast-but-ill-handling Mach II two stroke and later Honda's CB750 four.

Read Titan did not possess the resources or engineering expertise to completely replace the Honda's chassis, but it did prosper with its distinctive line of parts covering just about every other area of the big 750.

For around 1,000 pounds sterling (or roughly the cost of a new Honda CB750), a customer could transform an ordinary-looking CB into a sleek, stylish, and modern café racer that resembled a true paddock refugee. The model shown here was assembled during the early 1970s and later purchased disassembled and subsequently rebuilt by American café racer expert Robert Simpson. Simpson has also restored vintage café racers for motorcycle designer Craig Vetter.

This machine features Read Titan's distinctive full fairing with a set of Dunstall clip-on handlebars and matching Dunstall rear-sets. The Read Titan fuel tank holds 5 gallons of gas and is constructed from aluminum alloy, though a less expensive fiberglass model was also available.

The firm later abandoned manufacturing parts for British café racers altogether, focusing on the development of five-spoke alloy and magnesium wheels to replace the spoked items on this motorcycle. A matching tail section looks racy indeed, and that heavily padded saddle looks like something designed to protect a rider's valuables when forced against the tank during heavy braking. The Honda engine was bored out to 844cc, which is good for an additional 10 to 12 horsepower throughout the midrange. Its aspiration is helped through a four-into-one Kerker exhaust system with polished muffler and the overall performance of a Read Titan special helped along by the loss of 25 pounds in weight over the stock motorcycle.

1995 Triumph Speed Triple

Engine: Water-cooled, four-valve transverse triple
Displacement: 885cc
Power: 98 brake horsepower
Weight: 490 pounds
Top speed: 135 miles per hour

1995 TRIUMPH SPEED TRIPLE

Voted one of the Coolest Fifty Motorcycles of All Time by England's *Bike* magazine, one glance at Triumph's retro café racer proves why. For a modern, water-cooled motorcycle, the Speed Triple manages to affect a raw, café racer look that belies its mechanical modernity. The 885cc engine is kept smooth due to a pair of strategically placed countershafts, and the double overhead cams and twelve-valve heads sit atop pistons developed with help from Formula 1 engineers at Cosworth. The result is a thrilling, grunty ride, especially as the three massive cylinders begin to eat into their powerband that arrives with a satisfying whoosh around 7,000 rpm.

After its rebirth in 1991, there were other Triumph models, the Trophy and Daytona, that were meant to evoke images of the firm's hallowed past, but the Speed Triple was the first to do so successfully. Decked out in a moody, all-black finish, the Speed Triple's dark aura manages to hide the broad radiator hitched somewhat awkwardly to the front of the engine. A composite material seat hump manages to mimic the bum-stop racing saddle of the 1960s, and a set of high, rear-set foot controls and long, low clip-on handlebars show that this motorcycle means business.

For a somewhat weighty streetbike (460 pounds free of gas and oil) with a relaxed 27 degrees of rake, the Speed Triple was surprisingly quick to turn, prompting the formation of a single model

race series in the early 1990s. That was attributable to a set of fully adjustable 43-millimeter Kayaba forks, identical to those issued on the higher-performance, fully faired Daytona models. Japanese firm Nissin provided excellent stopping power via a set of four-piston front brake calipers mated to 320-millimeter full floating brake discs.

The Hinckley factory famously over-engineered 1990s Triumphs in an effort to make then unquestionably reliable, and it's not uncommon to see early Speed Triples looking fresh even with high five figures on the odometers. Some dedicated speed merchants have even stripped the fairings from Triumph's 1,200cc, four-cylinder Daytona of the early 1990s, christening the home-brewed naked roadster the Speed Quattro. It's a surprise the factory never ventured into this area. This was fire-breathing proof that the café racer market was craving a fresh take on the subject, which spawned a generation of neo-retro motorcycles.

1961 MANX NORTON

For a motorcycle considered the godfather of the café racer movement, few Manx Nortons actually were used to ride along Britain's public roads. Created and marketed principally to the professional, TT, and club racer markets, the Manx Norton was nevertheless a primary impetus for the whole ton-up movement. Whether in its 250cc, 350cc, or 500cc forms, this machine was considered quite revolutionary when introduced in 1950. With its dual, bevel-driven overhead camshafts (post-1952 500cc models only) the Manx (named in honor of the Isle of Man's indigenous populace) proved so formidable a competitor that racer Godfrey Nash managed to win the Yugoslav Grand Prix on one as late as 1969, six full years after Norton pulled the Manx from production.

Those and numerous other racing successes could be chalked up to the nimble little single's revolutionary Featherbed chassis, which proved far more stable in cornering than nearly any other chassis it raced against. The air-cooled single ran an 8.67:1 compression ratio, but a radical 13:1 piston was available for expert-class racers running alcohol-

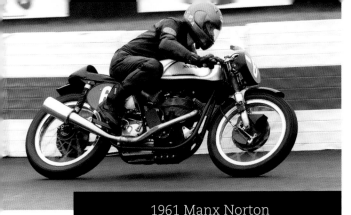

1961 Manx Norton

Engine: Air-cooled, DOHC bevel-drive single
Displacement: 499cc
Power: 37 brake horsepower
Weight: 298 pounds
Top speed: 130 miles per hour

cased fuels. The dry-sump engine produced 37.5 horsepower in stock form and ran a two-valve head. The Manx shifted with legendary ease thanks to a four-speed Norton transmission with a dry clutch with an exposed (and somewhat noisy) primary drive. At either end of the motorcycle's 56-inch wheelbase was top-quality running gear; Norton's legendary Roadholder forks provided stable cornering while a swingarm rear suspension offered 4 inches of travel.

With its magneto ignition providing just enough charge for the engine and not enough to run ancillary lighting, the Manx would have made an ill-equipped street machine, which is likely why so few appeared at the actual transport cafés. Far from cheap, most who could afford one were either factory-sponsored racers or those preferring to save their serious throttle

work for the track. And who could blame them for cherishing such a machine when demand for the Manx was always high and prices remained formidable as Norton was always awaiting back orders for frames that were slow to come from Reynolds Tube Company.

Today, the Manx remains perhaps the most valued British production café racer. Several firms produce complete replicas of the vaunted Manx Norton, constructed entirely of new parts. The most notable of these being Britain's Molnar Precision Limited, the firm that created the beautiful and ripping fast Molnar Manx replica raced by late GP champ Barry Sheene for several years at the annual Goodwood Festival of Speed.

1972 STEVE CARPENTER HONDA CB750

The arrival of large-displacement Japanese four-cylinder superbikes was greeted with a combination of suspicion and elation on both sides of the Atlantic during the early 1970s. At the time, the United States and Great Britain were home to motorcycle industries that were suffering from poor sales and backward-facing engineering techniques, causing many riders to look toward the Asian firms for new products. Though Britain's motorcycle performance aftermarket soon accepted the new in-line fours, creating an ample parts and accessories catalog to support them, Japanese motorcycles were considered a disposable commodity in the United States. That has only played into the hands of British expatriate Steve "Carpy" Carpenter who has developed a thriving cottage industry from these early 1970s

1972 Steve Carpenter Honda CB750

Engine: Air-cooled, two-valve SOHC transverse four
Displacement: 736cc
Power: 61 brake horsepower
Weight: 480 pounds
Top speed: 125 miles per hour

1977 Norton Commando John Player Special

Engine: Air-cooled, two-valve, parallel twin
Displacement: 745cc
Power: 55 brake horsepower
Weight: 399 pounds
Top speed: 120 miles per hour

Hondas, most of which have been cast-off into the hands of junk dealers and parts warehouses.

Carpy's specialty is rehabilitating these old, air-cooled Honda CB750 fours, a motorcycle the British-born craftsman says is among the best-handling, most powerful and reliable streetbikes ever made. The CB was futuristic with its five-speed gearbox, electric starter, and disc brakes, and therefore, designed to wear many hats, including commuter, tourer, and performance bike, which explains its neutral, unhurried steering and stout, double-cradle frame. However, the CB did not appear as a factory café racer until the arrival of the 1976 four-valve DOHC CB750F.

Carpenter's machine retains the factory chassis dimensions plus its stock, single overhead-cam, two-valve engine configuration of the early CB750, upgraded with a set of open-mouthed velocity stacks on the Kehin carburetors, and a four-into-two reverse megaphone exhaust. As a result, horsepower remains near the stock 67-brake horsepower figure, but Carpenter's machines move with a renewed urgency thanks to the utilization of several lightweight components.

Among them are racier fiberglass seats with custom upholstered leather saddles, fiberglass gas tanks that are stretched in length to better occupy the space between seat and headstock, and lightened fenders front and rear along with clubman bars. Carpenter likes to describe his café racer Hondas as "the motorcycle that Honda would have built had they listened to what their customers wanted," which is just about right.

1975 NORTON COMMANDO JOHN PLAYER SPECIAL

As the builder behind the legendary Manx Norton racing single, Norton was respected as a leader in the British motorcycle industry. It's Dominator and Atlas twins were capable, if not a bit staid-looking, machines that made fine café racers for thousands of riders during the 1960s. By that decade's end, however, Norton needed to up its game.

The stakes were raised with the arrival of Honda's CB450 twin and the CB750 four, both of which proved faster, more reliable, and smoother-running than anything wearing a Union Jack. Norton's design team struck back in 1969 with the 750cc Commando, a sleek-looking, low-profile machine wearing a futuristic tail section that bore a striking resemblance to a duck's bill. The Commando looked long thanks to its new bodywork, but at 56.8 inches the wheelbase had grown only an inch beyond that of the 1962 Atlas. The Commando may have looked odd, but it was a runner.

steel fuel tanks of the Atlas for a small, 3.9-gallon fiberglass fuel cell and a pair of mod torpedo-shaped mufflers. The Commando sold well on both sides of the Atlantic, with the John Player Special—named in honor of an experimental, monocoque-framed racer piloted by Peter Williams—spicing things up with special red-white-and-blue livery.

2003 KENNY DREER NORTON

Heralded in the U.S. magazine *Cycle World* as the next big thing in modern retro motorcycles, the Kenny Dreer Norton Commando was everything a café racer enthusiast could ever want. Based on a revamped, bored and stroked version of the legendary 850cc Norton Commando from the 1970s, the Dreer Norton displaced a hearty 952cc. The engine, first talked about with four overhead valves instead of the original Commando's two-valve configuration, was built entirely from new

The vibration issues that had plagued earlier Norton twins were addressed by an "Isolastic" engine-mounting system. Created by engineer Bernard Hooper, the system basically placed massive o-rings between engine, swingarm, and transmission bolts and the chassis. The frame was quite a departure from the Featherbed that had carried its previous generation twins, operating with a tubular steel, duplex-cradle design augmented with a single (and very rigid) top rail. The Isolastic bushings were wonderful for calming the 73x89-millimeter stroke engine, though they needed to be adjusted every 5,000 miles or the Commando's easy handling could be greatly compromised.

The Commando, which would see its displacement grow to 825cc by the late 1970s, also moved the game ahead by ditching the heavy

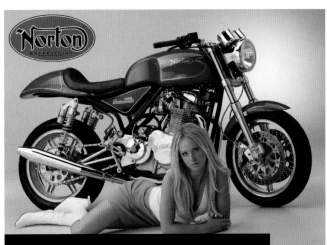

2003 Kenny Dreer Norton

Engine: Air-cooled, two-valve, parallel twin
Displacement: 952cc
Power: 90 brake horsepower
Weight: 415 pounds
Top speed: 145 miles per hour

parts with just two valves per cylinder, but offering vastly improved oil flow for additional cooling.

The bike's tubular frame was built from 4130 chromoly steel and reportedly was as effective as it was beautiful, capturing the classic lines of a café racer frame but offering modern, vibration-resistant rubber engine mounting points and a unique oil system that stored its 3.5 quarts of lubricant in the top frame rail. The dual rear shocks helped maintain the bike's classic appearance, but like the front end, they were to be manufactured by the Swedish top-shelf suspension firm Ohlins. This meant the Dreer Norton's suspenders offered more adjustment than an eight-armed chiropractor, while the 5.5 inches of front and 4.0 inches of rear-wheel travel were on par with modern superbikes.

The 5.5-inch rear and 3.5-inch-wide front wheels can be ordered in either carbon fiber or lightweight alloy, depending on the depth of a customer's pockets, and could accept the latest sticky radial tires. There's no wonder the cost of this motorcycle was estimated to be somewhere around $20,000 as Dreer, a former aerospace engineer with a taste for exotic café racers, equipped his machine with Brembo Gold Line brake calipers clutching 320-millimeter semi-floating rotors, a bespoke five-speed transmission, and modern instruments in a handsome brushed-alloy cluster. Test riders who were fortunate enough to bag a ride on one of these rare machines gushed about their near-perfect handling and the way the dry-sump, parallel twin engine made the most of its 80 brake horsepower.

The real key to enjoying this superb, lightweight roadster was by riding along in a single gear and relishing in the wads of torque that peaked at 65 foot-pounds at just 5,200 rpm.

Unfortunately, the public is still awaiting production models of Kenny Dreer's dream bike, now at 961cc, which has, to date, crept out of his Oregon workshop in only very limited numbers. Nevertheless, the Dreer Norton is one hell of a café racer.

1965 Velocette Venom Thruxton

Engine: Air-cooled two valve, pushrod single
Displacement: 499cc
Power: 40 brake horsepower
Weight: 395 pounds
Top speed: 105 miles per hour

1965 VELOCETTE VENOM THRUXTON
As the reborn Triumph concern would learn in the early twenty-first century, mining the hallowed racing circuits of Great Britain for commercial purposes is a wise policy. That's why Velocette (1904–1971) named its fastest production motorcycle after Thruxton, the Hampshire circuit where the firm enjoyed many of its racing victories. A marque long

1955 Vincent Series C Rapide

Engine: Air-cooled two-valve 50-degree V-twin
Displacement: 998cc
Power: 45 brake horsepower
Weight: 475 pounds
Top speed: 120 miles per hour

associated with an elegant, almost Victorian sense of design and high street style, the Velocette Thruxton actually descended from the sporty Venom single, which itself descended from the original 350cc single that catapulted racer Alec Bennett to a victory in the 1926 Junior TT on the Isle of Man. Continued racing success saw engine development at the Birmingham firm skyrocket through the 1940s and 1950s, culminating in the stylish and very quick 500cc Venom and 350cc Viper models of the 1950s.

As with most manufacturers conscious of the all-important links between racing and showroom traffic, Velocette offered the Venom single in Clubman form, appealing to café racers with its bum-stop seat, lightly souped-up engine, and (mercifully) uprated twin-leading shoe drum front brakes. The motorcycle could power along at 105 miles per hour in top gear.

By 1965, competition among British motorcycle manufacturers was at a peak, and Velocette again tapped into its rich racing heritage for the Thruxton, which was basically a Venom wearing lower, clip-on handlebars, Amal's Grand Prix carburetor in its single manifold, and an Avon fiberglass fairing. The Thruxton Venom would help shore up the firm's last four years of production by winning the 1967 500cc Production TT.

1954 VINCENT SERIES C RAPIDE

It took either deep pockets or fanatical dedication to ride a big Vincent twin during its heyday: In 1955, a Rapide cost roughly 420 pounds in the U.K., which is what many families paid for a semi-detached home. But few homes, it must be noted, were capable of whisking their owners through the ozone at 120 miles per hour, a figure considered otherworldly in an era when most production motorcycles struggled to break the ton.

Produced in Stevenage, England, the Vincent was not only fast, it was something akin to the oval-piston Honda NR750 what with its cutting-edge technology. The big, 998cc, 50-degree V-twin engine was utilized as a stressed member of the chassis, which helped keep weight comparable to that of far less powerful machines. The so-called Girdraulic forks installed on 1950s models were spindly for a motorcycle of such ferocious performance, but along with the dual, under-seat rear dampers, actually

1976 Laverda 1000 Jota

Engine: Air-cooled two-valve, DOHC transverse triple
Displacement: 981cc
Power: 90 brake horsepower
Weight: 520 pounds
Top speed: 140 miles per hour

provided a firm, predictable ride through corners. Twin drum brakes, however small, provided excellent stopping power, while the distinctive, long black fuel tank was designed to allow riders to stretch out prone to achieve maximum aerodynamics.

Of course, the Vincent's real appeal as a café racer came from its stunning straight-line speed, its legend helped along by American rider Rollie Free reaching the 150-mile-per-hour mark on a production Vincent Rapide during a long-distance run at the Bonneville Salt Flats in 1948. If there was a café racer truly deserving of the name Bonneville, perhaps this was it.

1976 LAVERDA 1000 JOTA

Dense, meaty, and imbued with muscular lines, the Laverda Jota was Italy's answer to the Norton Commando when released to critical acclaim in 1976. By this time, most mainstream manufacturers were cognizant enough of what sort of performance bikes their customers craved, and even the speed and technology-averse engineers at Harley-Davidson were entering the café racer game. The Jota, a 1000 triple, was based on Laverda's 750S and SF sportbikes from a few years earlier. Successful outings in European endurance racing with the very café'd SFC 750 parallel twin of 1972 and later had encouraged the company to explore the creation of larger-capacity engines for road use.

Laverda struck gold by producing a 981cc, three-cylinder, air-cooled powerplant featuring double overhead cams and a slick, five-speed gearbox. The 3C evolved into the Jota by 1975, which is renowned for its rawness and arm-stretching acceleration. No lightweight at 520 pounds full of fuel and lubricant, the Jota nevertheless produced a dizzying 90 brake horsepower, good for somewhere around 140 miles per hour. At the time, only Kawasaki's Z1 could achieve these levels of acceleration, and the handling of the big Kwacker always left much to be desired.

The Jota, on the other hand, shared that magical Italian ability to carve corners with courage, due to its strong, steel cradle frame, lightweight alloy wheels, and just plain fine engineering. So beloved was the big silver or orange Laverda triple that the company thought it could do no wrong. Sadly, the company's high production costs and iconic yet time wasting V-6 that took the majority of their development budget caught up with them. Production stopped.

**1977 Harley-Davidson
XLCR Café Racer**

Engine: Air-cooled, two-valve, OHV V-twin
Displacement: 1,000cc
Power: 55 brake horsepower
Weight: 490 pounds
Top speed: 120 miles per hour

1977 HARLEY-DAVIDSON XLCR CAFÉ RACER

The café racer craze that forever changed motorcycling overseas was slow to reach the United States. When the aftermarket finally did begin stocking bikini fairings, rear-sets, and clubman handlebars alongside extended chopper forks and ornate sissy bar backrests, it was only in small numbers to serve what never developed beyond a cult audience. Against this backdrop of uncertainty, it is ever harder today to discern the motivations behind the Harley-Davidson XLCR Café Racer (capitalization is emphasized, as this was the model's official name).

When introduced during the 1977 model year, the XLCR was as different from the remainder of the Milwaukee firm's line-up as Tritons are from choppers. Dressed up in cool black livery with an angular, coffin-shaped gas tank and wearing a set of very Japanese-looking side covers on the newly designed Sportster frame, the XLCR looked like a Batmobile in a barn full of 1957 Chevys. Testers have long argued over whether the XLCR was simply a styling exercise aimed at the wrong audience or a genuine attempt at building a high-performance production motorcycle. In reality, the machine represents a little of both schools.

Harley-Davidson did, after all, install a set of lightweight, five-spoke alloy wheels on the machine, along with a set of taller-than-usual rear shocks and a sinister-looking "Siamese" exhaust system. Though the 1,000cc (61-cubic-inch) pushrod-operated two-valve V-Twin engine remained in basically the same form it had since being introduced as a 55-cubic-inch model way back in 1957, the XLCR did sport the firm's first twin drilled disc brakes, and riders gripped a pair of flat, drag race–inspired handlebars behind a nifty bikini fairing. While the XLCR will never be remembered for its performance, it's become quite a collector's item due to its bold, unusual design.

5

Triton and Other Mongrels

For many, the amalgam of disparate parts that coalesced
into one-of-a kind custom café racers, also known
as specials, remains the heart and soul of the ton-up
movement. The long-term effects of the specials movement
cannot be overestimated when studying modern sportbikes,
as progress in chassis design can be directly attributed to
motorcycles built in garden sheds and small garages during
the 1950s and 1960s. Take the revered "factory specials"
proffered by Italy's Bimota, for example.

The company, founded in 1973 in Rimini, Italy,
on the eastern seaboard, by Messrs. Bianchi, Morri, and
Tamburini (hence, BiMoTa) were, like many café racers,
impressed by the performance capabilities of motorcycle

Page 122: *Original equipment still intact on this pre-unit Triton, built (for the first time, anyway) back in the early 1960s and still running today. Who says antique motorcycles aren't reliable?* Simon Green

engines available in the late 1960s but were equally appalled by the questionable handling. With an extensive roadracing and motorcycle engineering background shared by the trio of investors, their collective sights were set on drafting vastly improved frames for some of the fastest powerplants then available.

The original SB2, which cradled an air-cooled Suzuki GS750 engine in a revolutionary, lightweight tubular steel, monoshock chassis, was a watershed, hailed by the biking press as motorcycling's Great Leap Forward. Outfitted with twin front drilled disc brakes, Marzocchi racing forks, and a futuristic set of fairings that had a self-supporting subframe, the SB2 could hit 130 miles per hour and do so without scaring the rider into a new set of drawers when encountering tight

The Rickman brothers' frame concern made its reputation designing chassis for 1960s off-road racers, but their Metisse—a French slang term for a mongrel dog—café racer frame was among the finest available. Still in limited production, the Metisse Triumph offers Featherbed levels of handling with lightweight steel construction. Author's collection

corners. It was enough to spawn an entire bespoke motorcycle chassis revolution. There'd be no Harris or Spondon streetfighter specials without Bimota, but the formula—vulcanizing one manufacturer's chassis and bolting in a nonstock motor and top-level ancillaries—was perfected twenty years hence in Great Britain.

These early specials builders faced a challenging path as they forged their high-performance motorcycles with little more than guesswork and guile. There are as many schools of thought concerning what components and arrangements thereof make for a superior special as there are variations on the Featherbed-based custom. During the heyday of the Triton, a motorcycle some claim surfaced in primitive form as early as 1954, some veterans recall seeing Featherbed-equipped Triumph Speed Twins racing at British short circuits during that time. Mongrel motorcycles, as they were derisively labeled by some, were in many ways inevitable for a generation of enthusiasts determined to ride as quickly as possible.

By the mid-1950s, when Tritons first began to appear, a clear, unassailable hierarchy had developed among café racers, who saw obvious advantages and disadvantages among various machines. Triumph twins were clearly head and shoulders ahead of the pack when it came to outright speed and useable power, but their frames were less than enthusiastically received. BSA's 650cc Golden Flash of the early 1960s were handsome reliable bikes, but both the performance and handling was nothing to get excited about; big displacement twins like the Matchless G9, 500cc Super Clubman, and the AJS 30 CSR Sports Twin suffered from reliability problems considered unacceptable even for that repair-prone age, with a shared reputation for detonating occasionally if revved too hard at high speed.

Royal Enfield's biggest two-cylinder machines were known for similar reliability issues, including weak gearboxes, and offered unremarkable handling while Norton was known for manufacturing the world's best chassis with uninspiring looks and mediocre performance. The natural conclusion was to combine as many of the more desirable components from these machines as possible in a Frankenstein's laboratory kind of experiment. And like the good doctor, the path to enlightenment was littered with failures, frustrations, and more than a few horrific dust-ups between physics and reality. The Norton chassis was broad, tall, and deep enough in scale to accept just about any engine ever produced by a British motorcycle manufacturer, but placing said motors in a frame in a way that would allow them smooth operation and improved handling, for example, proved a matter of debate.

Some builders experimented with combining either 500cc or 650cc pre-unit Triumph twin engines with BSA's close-ratio gearboxes in Tritons, but getting these components to line up properly was the stuff of nightmares. The BSA transmissions bumped into frame gussets on the Norton Dominator Featherbed; without proper alignment, the gearboxes leaked oil liberally.

Some desperate owners spent months and many hundreds of pounds collecting the parts to build specials, only to find that their high-compression engines rattled loose or broke in two the engine-mounting lugs on some Featherbed frames, or that gearboxes had to be remounted so far forward in their new chassis they suffered from long, unruly chains that chewed through frame rails. The Featherbed's extreme length

Fine Noriel café racer special parked up at Brighton featuring a set of aluminum side covers and side-draft intakes on the quartet of Amal Concentric carburetors. Simon Green

also meant builders had to run far longer drive chains on their specials than on stock machines. These could sap horsepower and break easily over uneven pavement or under hard acceleration. Front ends that were too long caused oil-starvation problems as the special ended up sitting low in the rear and high in the front while too short a front end meant steering that was quick, or too quick in some situations.

Countless specials builders became fast friends with their local machinists and lathe operators as fork stanchions were cut and re-cut for size and frame lugs welded and replaced when drilling holes turned up the wrong size or in the wrong place.

Wiring was also a potential minefield for the amateur specials builder as there were no aftermarket wiring diagrams to be downloaded on a nonexistent internet in those days, and there were few ways to master the tricky Lucas electrical

Dave Degens talks shop with one of his many customers during the 1960s Triton heyday. Degens has built hundreds of the specials and is considered the greatest living café racer engineer. Author's collection

An engineering challenge indeed, which is why Trident T140 specials owners are so proud of their motorcycles. Mounting the three-cylinder Triumph Trident engine within the tight confines of a Featherbed takes serious perseverance. Bauer Media

John Mossey's Egli-Vincent characterized by a stump-pulling 1,200cc engine featuring electric starting and modern crankcases with five-speed gearbox. JMR photo

systems other than trial and error. Lucky for some, the pre-unit Triumph engines used in many a mongrel operated on simple, magneto-powered ignition systems, which made wiring a trouble-free affair. In those days, motorcycles frequently ran on the streets with only the barest auxiliary lighting equipment, so attaching a tiny, friction-powered headlight and taillight could get a rider past all but the most circumspect traffic patrolmen.

But like most mechanical experiments, time and experience quickly resolved these dilemmas, and as a result, a folk knowledge of what worked and what didn't when building a mongrel machine surfaced in the café racer community. Friends who had successfully completed fast, sharp-handling machines out of parts were held in high regard by their peers, who could be counted on to besiege the successful for tuning tips. Home-spun Tritons were created by the likes of Allen Dudley-Ward, who for a time experimented with running his Triumph engine heads backwards in hopes of improving cylinder cooling. Dudley-Ward was a sought-after tuner who later perfected the high-level dual exhaust system. Other notable specials builders included Ian Kennedy, who built a small industry offering complete, made-to-order Tritons and the necessary bits for home specials jobs as well.

In time, riders learned that all of those high-compression, track-proven motors they'd lusted after tended to run hotter and less reliably in town and were bastard tough to kickstart on a cold night down the caff. Open bellmouths on a carburetor looked just like the set-ups favored by Grand Prix racers, but they tended to make carbs run on the rich side and dirt and other debris could easily find its way inside an open carb. BSA gearboxes proved equally unnecessary as the mild state of tune and easy rideability of a Triumph T110 or T120 twin meant the stock transmission worked well enough on its own. Some of the more gifted specials builders fitted complex superchargers that could catapult a twin into velocities known only to jet test pilots, but given the limits of tire technology at the time, it's no surprise these contraptions were not more widely used.

smart with their chromed springs but provided increased ride height over stock suspenders, while lightweight headlamp brackets, fenders, and a host of other accessories soon came to codify the Triton as solidly as two-tone paint and reserved good taste characterized a Triumph Bonneville. The mounting of ancillaries such as clip-ons and rear-sets or the question of whether to run an alloy or new fiberglass gas or oil tank is still hotly debated among specials builders, though these issues are all down to a matter of individual taste.

Akront alloy rims laced to original hubs and, when they could be sourced from a junkyard, Norton Roadholder forks were almost universally agreed upon as *the* items for any special, as the forks, with their stiff spring and double-damping rates were superior to much on the market at that time. Girling shock absorbers not only looked

Building a Truly Special Special

Just as there's no one roadracer considered the best of all time—some prefer Hailwood's upright, devastatingly quick cornering style while others find Ago's flamboyant moves more to their liking—a consensus on what combination of go-fast components makes the perfect café racer is a matter of fierce debate. Over the years, entire thesauruses have been ravaged in search of the proper words to describe the handling of 1960s Nortons, but there are just as many committed fans of Norton's Commando from the 1970s. For everyone extolling the virtues of the Featherbed chassis, there's a specials enthusiast who can tell of corners taken on a Harris Magnum or early Bimota that were transcendent in their perfectness.

The mere act of swapping a set of forks designed for a motorcycle to a pair from an entirely different brand could immeasurably ruin or complement a machine's cornering skills, just as mounting an engine too far forward or rearward in a new chassis would prove a motorcycle's downfall or triumph.

Likewise, many purists who cut their teeth on British-made parallel twins will turn their collective noses up at the thought of riding a motorcycle powered by an in-line four-cylinder powerplant of Japanese origin. While both types of machine offer their own advantages both aesthetically and in the realm of performance, the twins did, in this writer's humble opinion, enjoy a certain historical appeal, not to mention a timeless look due to their large, air-cooling fins, exposed pushrod valve-actuating gear, and a decent level of easy-to-utilize (if not a bit underwhelming) power. On the contrary, specials built around the responsive, 70-horsepower Honda CB750 engines from the early 1970s have made a strong comeback, particularly in the U.S. market where the engines tend to be cheap, reliable, and easily tuned for more power.

Though the meaty four-cylinder Honda powerplant provided loads of smooth, dependable power, it never looked quite right shoehorned into a specials chassis where it tended to dwarf all the other components. During the 1970s, famed British tuner and specials builder Paul Dunstall made some impressive strides turning CB750, and later CB500, Hondas into genuine café racers, offering owners high-compression piston kits made from a special low-expansion, high-silicon content material that, with their higher-than-stock 10.25:1 compression ratio, made for more efficient CB750 engines that ran faster than anyone expected.

Dunstall also offered half-fairing kits for the big Hondas, following suit with plenty of fiberglass accessories for the 900cc, and later 1,000cc Kawasaki fours. Like all the early Japanese superbikes, handling was always an issue and simply adding more power to these already formidable machines could be a one-lane road to disaster when the motorcycles' engines could so easily overpower their chassis.

To address those shortcomings, firms such as Rickman Engineering, run by brothers Derek and Don, offered full, upgraded chassis to suit the big Japanese fours. They may have been expensive, but the Rickman chassis were a revelation, transforming the CB750 from a delicate sport-touring machine into a winning club racer.

One of my favorite specials ever was spotted at the Isle of Man TT along the busy Douglas Promenade; built from a Wideline Featherbed chassis and housing a Suzuki GSX-R 750 engine, it was drawing more than its share of attention, which is no easy task in a bike-mad place like the Isle of Man. The owner had followed an interesting approach in building this particular machine, equipping his special with ultra-modern amenities, including upside-down 43-millimeter Showa forks, full-floating stainless steel disc brakes, and a beautifully engineered mounting system for an Ohlins monoshock. The café racer, when viewed from a glance, still appeared to have rolled intact straight out of the 1960s due to its Manx-pattern allow gas tank, tiny, bum-stop seat, and shorty alloy fenders.

It's this melding of the classic and the modern that's one of the greatest joys of specials building as there really aren't any rules except to build a motorcycle that's at once more beautiful and more exhilarating to ride than any other. Truth be told, café racers, being mostly specials, customs, and one-off machines, are all subjective when it comes to what makes them tick.

Faired Dresda Triton wears the classic silver, black, and red livery of the Manx Norton and bears many of Dave Degens's signature modifications, including fold-away footpegs fixed directly to the engine mounting plates and reverse-pattern gear lever. Author's collection

The master, Dave Degens, admires his handiwork since first marrying a Norton chassis with a tuned Triumph motor in the late 1950s.

Dave Degens, perhaps the best-known specials builder, has his own theories on how the whole Triton game got its launch and how a sometimes confused custom motorcycle developed a unified style. "A gang of us used to hang out in a café, the Queen of Hearts between Twickenham and Hounslow (not far from London's Heathrow airport). I had a rigid 350 Matchless on the road, but a friend, Johnny Gray, put a Triumph Tiger 110 engine in a Featherbed frame. He kept the Norton gearbox and ran an open primary chain. It was virtually a racing bike with lights," he recalled years later.

Degens, who later went on to form Dresda Autos, producers of some of the most elegant, hard-riding café racers in existence, was smitten with that first hybrid Britbike. His admiration was forever cemented when his own mount broke down one evening only to have Triton pioneer Johnny Gray tow Degens and his disabled motorcycle the entire distance from Salisbury to London, and at 75 miles per hour yet! By 1958, after a stint racing and then repairing BSAs for friend Monty Black's dealership, Degens started building tritons of his own. The opportunity presented itself in the form of a Manx Norton wheeled into the shop with a blown engine, which Degens rebuilt with a T120 Triumph motor. The motorcycle sold immediately, he remembered, and soon he was busy perfecting the machines that would become synonymous with café racer specials.

At one point during the 1960s, Dresda Autos employed a full-time staff of a nearly dozen to handle the frantic demand for their custom café racers. Today, Degens remains busy, hand-building each machine that bears the Dresda marque. Bauer Media

At one point, specials were so popular in the U.K., that Degens's shop was employing five full-time assembly workers who toiled for the Gods of Speed to the tune of fifty hours each week. Most customers favored the wide-line Featherbed chassis, which was broad enough across the waist to cause discomfort for smaller pilots, but offered

Looking primed and ready for the road, this looker of a 1965 Triton roars away thanks to a T120 unit construction motor. Over the years, some preservationists have lamented the popularity of specials which depleted the stocks of OEM machines. Bauer Media

such superior handling to frames from Triumph, Matchless, or BSA, that Triton customers were willing to suffer. Degens figures they built around 700 Tritons—some naked, some sporting stylish half-fairings, and one of a half-dozen variations on seats, handlebar height, and engine specs—before Wideline chassis (which were supplanted by the Slimline version in 1960s) became thin on the ground.

A certain urgency left the specials scene with the arrival of the Norton Dominator of 1965, which wasn't a bad-looking machine and, being based on a Featherbed, handled nicely. Triumph's twin-carbureted, unit-construction Bonneville of the mid-1960s was also a fair-handling motorcycle, which many potential Triton customers found it easier to buy than mucking about trying to collect the necessary bits (not to mention the needed expertise) to complete a special on their own. A brilliant draftsman and engineer, Degens eventually developed his own variation on the Wideline chassis, improving the welded-on engine mounting lugs (which could break off in poorly built specials) and nickel-plating the frames to withstand the ravages of a typical British winter.

During the 1970s, Degens and other specials shops turned their attentions to the growing demand for uprated running gear for the emergent Japanese four-cylinder machines. These bikes required far stiffer chassis to accommodate the

raw, top-end power of an in-line four, and as they arrived in showrooms shorn of any recognizable style of their own, seemed to be begging for dropped bars, café seats, and the usual footlocker full of bolt-on, go-fast accessories. The first Dresda Honda CB750s were revealed at the 1970 London Motorcycle Show and proved an instant hit. Many riders who had spent years constructing mongrel motorcycles out of British stock were reluctant to embrace the new imported machines, which undeniably offered superior performance to the parallel twins, including Norton's rubber-mounted and very modern-looking Commando 750. That all began to change as specials experts like Colin Seeley, the Rickman Brothers, and Paul Dunstall switched their energies to making true café racers from Hondas, and later Kawasakis.

Though few, if any of the original home-brew specials makers are still in the game, it is a pleasure to know that Rickman's original Metisse frames are still being produced by a small concern in the rural hamlet of Carswell, Oxfordshire, England. The line of sleek, oil-in-frame Metisse chassis now includes kits to turn a Harley-Davidson Sportster into a mongrel machine, as well as a faithful reproduction of the popular 1960s Metisse café racer, complete with the chromoly steel frame carrying the engine oil inside, a fiberglass box-shaped gas tank, racing seat, and just about anything else aimed at making a modern café racer enthusiast feel like a genuine ton-up boy.

The popular Dunstall kits for Japanese bikes available during the 1970s are now rare and highly valuable collectors items, even though aesthetically, they lacked the flowing lines and tidy dimensions of his Norton Domiracers from a decade previous due to the larger dimensions of the Japanese machines. But like all mongrels, they handled admirably, eliminating that spooky, midcorner flex that unnerved many a Honda CB750 owner at the time. This second generation of specials ran for a period that ended in the late 1970s, a time by which the Japanese manufacturers were finally exhibiting an ability to manufacture frames that worked nearly as good as their engines.

Revving your Triton at Brighton; the café racer scene could not have prospered and persevered without meetings like the annual Southend Shakedown where valuable technical information changes hands. Simon Green

By the start of the next decade, the first monoshock-equipped, perimeter frame sportbikes were rolling out of Honda's factory in the form of the original V45 Interceptors (though Bimota's SB2 had done so a decade earlier), and their influence on motorcycle design would soon make the need for bespoke chassis less immediate than at any other time since the inception of the café racer. But the mongrel bikes developed a permanent place in motorcycling's history and proved that specials will always be the heart and soul of the café racer scene, regardless of their country of origin.

Building a Triton: A Recipe Distilled

There is good reason that specials experts like Dave Degens of London's Dresda Autos receives orders for his home-brewed motorcycles from collectors and racers from around the globe; he's damn good at his job. Years in the specials business has taught Degens the ins and outs of café racer building on a level most mortals can only ascribe to. When attempting to construct my own Triton from an amalgam of parts, some new, some not so new, I encountered myriad unforeseen problems that took some trial, lots of error, and more than a little money to sort out in the end.

Building a café racer is a thrilling, deeply satisfying experience as is riding one on modern roads; however, there are a few points the novice should heed as the classified ads are full of uncompleted project bikes. For starters, it's important to select the components that you ultimately want to see on your machine from the very start, even if it means postponing the completion of the project until all funds are in place. Antique motorcycles are notorious for their vibration, especially at speed, so be prepared to have some teeth-rattling moments with a special. The alloy engine mounting plates that permit an oddball engine to mount in a Featherbed frame only add to the equation, as they place the engine's steel crankcase directly in contact with the chassis, transferring loads of vibration to footpegs, fenders, and other far-mounted ancillaries. That means using plenty of thread-locking compound and checking bolts regularly.

Also, because the featherbed is more than capable of providing excellent handling with a stock displacement British twin engine, I'd advise against attempting to build a high-compression, track-ready monster without the help of a real expert. Lumpy cams and ported heads with oversized valves in bronze guides may sound impressive in the paddock, but for everyday reliability, I'd choose to run with a restored, clean Triumph T120 Bonneville engine, or even better, a Kawasaki W650 engine for miles of trouble-free café racer riding.

1970s Rob North Norton Commando

Engine: Air-cooled, two-valve, parallel twin
Displacement: 750cc
Power: 52 brake horsepower
Weight: 390 pounds
Top speed: 120 miles per hour

1970'S ROB NORTH NORTON COMMANDO

Specials builder Rob North started out in the U.K. building Tribsa hybrids and Tritons during the 1960s, but by the mid-1970s, North, a gifted engineer and racer, had developed his own ideas about what made motorcycles lighter, faster, and sleeker. The result was the Rob North Commando, a café racer built around North's own, twin-cradle, triangular chassis. North's frame was a notable improvement over the stock Commando's chassis, which was better suited to touring duties than aggressive cornering or racetracks. He'd reached similar conclusions when BSA introduced its Rocket 3 back in the late 1960s.

North's ideas proved so effective, that the Triumph and BSA machines racing at Daytona during the late 1960s all rolled on his frames, not factory designs. Though he built racing machines bearing all manner of high-performance upgrades, North knew that dropping massive amounts of weight was the quickest, and cheapest, means of making a stock-engine café racer faster. North also designed aluminum gas tanks and fenders to complement his flex-free frames. This machine sports an aggressive-looking alloy tail section riding over the boxed-section swingarm. Triple Lockheed disc brakes were standard on the North Commando, as were open belt drives, which also helped reduce overall weight. North would later design Triumph's oil-in-frame chassis for the 1971 and later T140 Bonnevilles, before retiring to California, where he continued to build specials for several years.

1990 LANCE WEIL HARLEY-DAVIDSON FEATHERBED SPECIAL

As one of the last of his generation of American roadracers to compete in Great Britain during the 1960s, Pennsylvanian Lance Weil was committed to combining the best elements of motorcycles from each side of the Atlantic. His Featherbed Sportster provided inspiration for many café racers over the years, as the long, 60-degree Milwaukee engine proved a perfect, if not difficult to install, fit for the Featherbed. Weighing a scant 354 pounds, the Weil Special used a 3.75-gallon alloy gas tank, fiberglass fenders, and a matching half-fairing. Forks were Italian Marzocchi 38-millimeter models, considered the gold standard for front suspension at the time, while Akront's lightweight wire wheels with drum brakes front and rear revealed a penchant for acceleration but not much stopping power.

During competition, Weil's Harley-Davidson ran a primitive Morris Magneto ignition system, open "drag" exhaust pipes, and an open-mouthed, 44-millimeter S&S carburetor. As a result, the motorcycle was as renowned for its speed as it was for its distinctive sound. When Weil retired and began offering limited-production versions of his fabled Anglo-American racer through his California shop Ricky Racer for $34,000 each, Weil had tamed the beast a bit, installing working mufflers and a modern electrical system. Weil was tragically killed in a workshop accident in 2006, but his machines are being resurrected by a team led by Ace Café London owner Mark Wilsmore and custom motorcycle designer Nick Gale, who plan to release a limited-production run of the machines with modern, S&S V-twin engines.

1990 Lance Weil Harley-Davidson Featherbed Special

Engine: Air-cooled, two-valve 60-degree V-twin
Displacement: 61 cubic inches (1,000cc)
Power: 60 brake horsepower
Weight: 354 pounds
Top speed: 120 miles per hour

2007 VON DAZ T150 TRITON

Though the heart and legacy of the café racer special lives in England, the café racer cult has a strong following in Australia, a place where sunny weather and long, empty roads has attracted its share of British motorcyclists. Custom motorcycle builder Von Daz handcrafted this rare Triton from a Slimline Featherbed frame and a Triumph Trident three-cylinder engine, a combination the West Sydney native says produces all the fine handling and twice the power of a twin. The T150 engine was seldom used in café racer specials due to its additional weight and complexity over a twin, but some specials builders enjoy the

2007 Von Daz T150 Triton

Engine: Air-cooled, two-valve,
transverse three-cylinder
Displacement: 750cc
Weight: 376 pounds
Top speed: 125 miles per hour

2004 Baines Racing Ducati Project Imola

Engine: Air-cooled, two-valve 90-degree V-twin
Displacement: 900cc
Power: 73 brake horsepower
Weight: 419 pounds
Top speed: 135 miles per hour

challenges of the larger powerplant, which offers superior performance on every level.

The 1963 Norton Atlas frame was cut and widened to make room for the central oil tank, while the five-speed transmission shifts gears through a reverse-mounted shifter pedal for a one-up, four-down gear-change pattern. The engine breathes through a trio of 28-millimeter Mikuni carburetors, with the fumes exiting via a set of reverse megaphone exhausts. The Norton Roadholder forks with chromed, exposed springs are a café racer classic, as is the low-boy Norton Domiracer-style fiberglass gas tank. Fenders are alloy Manx replica models, covering a 19-inch Akront valanced front-spoked wheel with a twin leading-shoe front brake from a 1968 Triumph Bonneville, the rear being a later conical version. Installing a T150 triple into a Featherbed is no game for amateurs, as only 6 millimeters of clearance were left between the top of the engine head and the bottom of the crankcase. None of the engine's top-end maintenance can be performed without first removing the entire powerplant from its moorings, for example. Still, for originality and outright speed, few specials can match a Trident Triton.

2004 BAINES RACING DUCATI PROJECT IMOLA

Veteran Ducati tuner John Baines, like most café racers, reveres the original Ducati 750SS but is aware of how difficult it is to attain one. Baines, who has tuned several British Supersport teams, came upon a classic specials builder's solution to the scarcity of genuine early Supersport machines: He designed a DIY kit for home builders. The Baines Racing Project Imola is a clever take on the Italian steed, allowing late-model Ducati Supersport motorcycles to be reincarnated as a spitting image of the 1972 race winner. The kit includes a chassis, welded in Baines' own jigs, that allows the modern SS, air-cooled two-valve engine (whether it's a 1,000 Dual Spark, 900, 800 or 750cc variety) to be bolted right into place, using most of the stock ancillaries, including the airbox, forks, wheels, footrests, lighting equipment, and brakes. Changes include a switch to twin-shock rear suspension and the addition of a 3.2-gallon alloy gas tank that's hidden beneath an Imola replica fiberglass shell.

With their relatively simple two-valve heads and air-cooled aluminum cylinders, the modern Ducati Supersports are tunable motorcycles, responding well to lumpy cams, drop-in piston kits from the likes of Fast By Ferracci or even complete big bore kits that stretch a 900cc model into a ripping 944cc monster. However, John Baines says the machine is at its best in stock form where the 73 horses provide enough stomp to move the motorcycle along gracefully. Baines has sold several hundred of his kits and many of the owners eagerly share photos of their completed project Imola bikes on the internet. With such fine, classic café racer lines, the machines look good whether wearing the Baines half-fairing or naked in the form of Ducati's fabulous, bright yellow 750 Sport of 1974.

2007 RICKMAN KAWASAKI W650

The motorcycle press has been almost united in its praise of Kawasaki's retro W650, a motorcycle that some say out Bonnevilles' Triumph's own retro Bonneville in the looks department. The W650 actually mines Kawasaki's own heritage, harking back to the W1 parallel twin introduced by the Hamamatsu firm in 1968. The new machine has developed a faithful cult following in Europe, and particularly Germany where this bike calls home. This machine is a stunning example of old-meets-new as the owner managed to shoehorn the bevel-drive Kawasaki engine into an oil-in-frame Rickman Metisse café racer chassis originally designed to hold a BSA Lightning motor.

Needless to say, the Kawasaki's dimensions so faithfully follow earlier British engineering dimensions that, using just a set of specially made welded-on engine mounts, the transformation to true mongrel status was achieved. Look closely and you'll spot the Kawa's stock rubber front engine mount still in place, an accessory the owner retained to ward off the twin's notorious vibration. The benefits of this costly and time-consuming exercise is a machine that looks like something from the

Busy Bee Café parking lot forty years ago, but offers modern reliability, fabled Rickman handling, and, thanks to some very sexy hand-pounded aluminum alloy bodywork from Rickman's 1960s catalog, great looks as well. A nice touch is the fiberglass half fairing originally designed for a Ducati 900SS and the rounded alloy tail section and racing seat.

Not much of the Kawasaki's original running gear survived the custom job, as a set of forks from a Suzuki Bandit were bolted into one-off alloy fork yokes, replacing the Kawasaki's relatively weak, single disc brake with a set of dual, four-piston Nissin calipers. The Suzuki's brakes, however, were mated to the Kawasaki's stock wire rims, which add a cool period look to the machine. The owner has added an oil cooler to aid high-speed performance and a set of stubby, clip-on handlebars, but he kept the stock center stand. This proves the W650 café racer is still a practical, everyday machine.

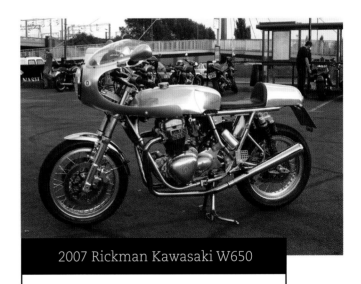

2007 Rickman Kawasaki W650

Engine: Air-cooled, two-valve,
    bevel-drive parallel twin
Displacement: 650cc
Power: 45 brake horsepower
Weight: 465 pounds
Top speed: 125 miles per hour

2007 Hailwood Motorcycle Restorations Norvin

Engine: Air-cooled two-valve, 47.5-degree V-twin
Displacement: 998cc
Power: 51 brake horsepower
Weight: 414 pounds
Top speed: 129 miles per hour

2007 HAILWOOD MOTORCYCLE RESTORATIONS NORVIN

Easily the most beloved and most controversial café racer conversion, the forced marriage of the Featherbed frame with engines from the HRD Vincent line is a hybrid machine that continues to divide classic bike enthusiasts. Vincents were always costly, exotic machines, attracting a clientele that were as far removed culturally and socially from the ton-up scene as one could get. Home-brewed café racers were generally built by speed merchants who admired the Vincent's cutting-edge technology and top-speed figures, but had little patience for the gentlemanly, pipe-and-slippers crowd they attracted.

None of that matters today when Norvins are viewed as brilliant examples of the specials builder's can-do attitude and the determination it took to make such a hybrid motorcycle work at all. For starters, the 998cc Vincent V-twin was almost too large to fit within the confines of a Featherbed frame; many chassis had their top frame rails cut in order to make room for the front carburetor, which weakened the chassis considerably. Some were forced to remove frame sections during engine mounting, securing the Vincent lump into place and then rewelding the rails as the special neared completion. This Norvin is based on a Manx Replica chassis with the front frame downtubes removed: In their stead the Vincent motor is bolted directly to the chassis's top rails, utilizing the engine as a stressed frame member just as the engineers at Vincent did. The routing of oil lines, electrical components, and even adjusting the valves became a chore for Norvin builders, but with razor-sharp cornering and a 130-mile-per-hour potential as their reward, many felt the effort to be more than worthwhile.

David Hailwood, son of 1960's champion GP racer Mike "The Bike" Hailwood took control of the former John Mossey Restorations in Northamptonshire, England in early 2008. A dedicated vintage bike enthusiast, Hailwood set about perfecting the recipe for a multi-bike line of bespoke machines including this retro Norvin. Built in either 998cc or 1,200cc versions, both equipped with electric starter, dual Dell'Orto carburetors and five-speed, close-ratio gearbox, the HMR Norvins are a worthy modern recreations of a classic café racer. Italian Ceriani forks of 40mm and four leading shoe Menani front brake help this machine to ride faster and stop more quickly than did most Norvins from a half century earlier.

Engine: Air-cooled, two-valve parallel twin
Displacement: 650cc
Power: 42 brake horsepower
Weight: 380 pounds
Top Speed: 120 miles per hour

1998 DRESDA TRITON

Dave Degens, builder of this classic Triumph-Norton hybrid, has so perfected his café racer formula that this machine could easily be mistaken for one of the motorcycles the West London shop produced nearly a half century ago. However, constant research and development and years of riding and designing Featherbed-based specials have imbued this motorcycle with a host of performance enhancements. With the world's stock of original Norton chassis very low, the frame, for example, is a Degen's Wideline replica, built with improved engine mounts and a box-section swingarm to accept modern radial tires. Weighing just 23 pounds, it's a replica of the original Manx chassis and maintains that machine's flawless handling characteristics. Dresda's own alloy top fork clamps provide room for a set of original Smith's instruments that are mounted between a set of swan's neck Dresda clip-ons. Taller than even a set of clubman bars, they manage to look stylish while providing light flickable steering.

The rear hub is a BSA conical model of 1960s vintage, though that's a Fontana four leading shoe front drum, manufactured recently but designed—from its mesh cooling screen to its mock-bronze finish—to look antique. The front end is another Dresda original, manufactured in-house using a combination of British motorcycle front ends from the 1960s and aluminum lowers and exposed chromed springs. An open belt drive powers the four-speed Triumph gearbox mated to a rebuilt T120 unit engine mounted using plates constructed from 1/4-inch Dural alloy. Up and sprinting along a deserted country lane, the riding sensation on a Dresda Triton is said to be the reason the term *Featherbed* was coined.

1995 UNITY EQUIPE TRITON

Unity Equipe is a Lancashire, England-based specials parts firm with a long history of supplying Triton builders. For a time during the 1970s, the firm held production rights to the Manx Norton, which permitted Unity's staff ample time to experiment with hard parts for go-fast classic motorcycles, including strengthened and updated Featherbed frames complete with box-section swingarms capable of accommodating rear disc brakes and wider radial tires. This Triton was built almost entirely from Unity's catalog, where the 6-gallon alloy, Manx-style gas tank, Converta engine

1995 Unity Equipe Triton

Engine: Air-cooled, two-valve, parallel twin
Displacement: 650cc
Power: 46 brake horsepower
Weight: 395 pounds
 Top speed: 115 miles per hour

mounting plates, swept-back exhaust pipes with 3 3/4-inch reverse megaphone mufflers, and hump-backed seat were sourced. Built by Collin's Cycle, a Pittsburgh-area Triumph dealership, the machine features a set of forks from a T120 Triumph Bonneville, which supplied the front and rear wheels as well.

The T120 unit engine was once used to power a stretch chopper the author used to commute on, despite its overly long springer forks and under-damped rear end! The Triton was built around a 1962 Norton Atlas Slimline Featherbed chassis that retained the stock oil tank on the right-hand side; the builder had never before (or since) tackled a café racer project of this complexity, but was clever enough to wrap the top twin frame rails in plumbing insulation to ward off stress fractures in the fuel tank. Brakes were single leading shoe conical units from a 1960s Triumph, while the ace or clubman handlebars were somewhat less cruel to my 6-foot 4-inch frame than a set of actual clip-ons might have been. Though Unity will build customers a complete, running special from their vast parts catalog, this machine shows that DIY builders can achieve admirable results on their own.

1972 Rickman CR750 Honda

Engine: Air-cooled, two-valve, SOHC transverse
      four cylinder
Displacement: 750cc
Power: 70 brake horsepower
Weight: 475 pounds
Top speed: 125 miles per hour

1972 RICKMAN CR750 HONDA

For their first two decades in production, little could be said about the handling prowess of the first generation of Japanese big-bore fours, except that it needed improvement. With their eye on the future, many British café racer specialists read the writing on the wall suggesting British motorcycles would soon be replaced by their Asian peers. Among the first to do so was the Rickman Brothers who had been designing and manufacturing chassis kits and engine components since the early 1960s. A one point, it was estimated that around half of the off-road motorcycles competing in the U.K. did so using Rickman-Metisse (clever use of a French term for female mongrel!) frames, which were available along with forks, bodywork kits, and anything else a racer desired.

Honda's CB750 first hit the streets in 1969, and it took the Rickman Brothers just more than a year to complete the CR (for *café racer*, naturally), a full, makeover for the popular machine. This one is done up in a lively bright orange and features Don and Derek Rickman's alloy trellis, nickel-plated frame along with Girling rear shock

absorbers, Rickman's own forks and wheels, plus a sporty tail section that reveals a direct design lineage between the original hump-backed café racer seats of the early era and the fiberglass tail enclosures still used on sportbikes today.

The tasty front fairing was clearly inspired by Dunstall's ideas, and the long, flat gas tank was perfect for flat-out acceleration. The CB750 makeover was similar to the kits offered to British specials builders as some of the stock accessories such as instruments, exhausts, and electrics could still be used to keep customer costs down. But for the cash, the Rickman CR750 showed that Japanese motorcycles could look good and traverse corners as well as anything.

2002 GODET EGLI-VINCENT

French specials wizard Patrick Godet has a case full of trophies to show for his work improving on Swiss designer Fritz Egli's vision of the perfect high-end café racer. During the 1960s, Egli became synonymous with the Vincent marque

2002 Godet Egli-Vincent

Engine: Air-cooled two-valve, 47.5-degree V-twin
Displacement: 998cc
Power: 65 brake horsepower
Weight: 379 pounds (dry)
Top speed: 130 miles per hour

as his small-batch frame and running gear kits granted the 1950s V-twin something of a rebirth in the café racer scene. In recent years, the Egli name has carried on under Godet's tutelage, with a new generation of high-end specials incorporating the short-wheelbase, quick-steering designs that Egli perfected some forty years ago.

This Godet Egli-Vincent is typical of the machines churned out by the French factory at the rate of roughly one per month. An engine built for longevity is equipped with low-compression pistons and a Francois Grosset electric starting system that eliminated the need for a kickstart, as Godet's machines have fully modernized, 12-volt electrics, including a Boyer ignition kit. The rear-set footrests and clip-ons are reworked Vincent items, bolted to the oil-bearing chassis built to Egli's original specifications.

Front suspension consists of a set of Ceriani racing forks with a Fontana four leading shoe drum brake. In the rear, dual shocks from England's Maxton suspension handle the bumps. Vincent connoisseurs will notice a clever remounting of both 30-millimeter Amal concentric carburetors on the left side of the engine, which is a Godet specialty. His own two-into-one exhaust system, built to resemble that of a vintage BSA Gold Star, graces the right side of the machine, which also has Godet's original seat and gas tank attached. On the road, these powerful, torque-crazy machines are said to offer the most exciting ride among modern specials.

Egli started out designing a one-off frame that would help his own Vincent climb steep mountain roads. The result is a chassis with a wonderful "glued to the pavement feel," though the hefty $30,000 price tag means Godet's Egli-Vincent will remain an object of desire for more riders than it is a reality.

1991 GOODMAN HDS (HARLEY-DAVIDSON SPECIAL)

Though an undeniable sales flop in the Harley-mad United States, the short-lived XLCR Café Racer was something of a sensation in the U.K. and Europe. The XLCR's performance never matched its looks, however, prompting many specials builders to re-examine the American V-twin's café racer potential. In 1990, a small Worcestershire, U.K., concern known as Goodman Engineering introduced its limited-edition café racer built around the beefy, 74-cubic inch Harley-Davidson Sportster engine. The powerplant had much to offer a café racer with its prodigious

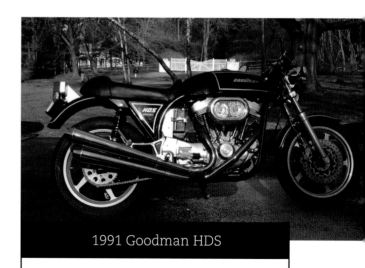

1991 Goodman HDS

Engine: Air-cooled, pushrod-operated V-Twin
Displacement: 1,200cc
Power: 55 brake horsepower
Weight: 489 pounds
Top speed: 118 miles per hour

torque (some 60 foot-pounds just off idle) and a throbby, reassuring feel despite its relatively low top speed of just under 120 miles per hour.

The Goodman was ripe with top-class components, including Brembo four-piston front brake calipers and the firm's own lightweight twin exhaust system. Handled far better than any production Harley-Davidson streetbike thanks to its chassis, fashioned from 531 Reynolds manganese-molybdenum carbon steel tubing and modeled on, what else but, the Norton Featherbed. The Goodman chassis featured something called Metalsilk rubber bushings designed to stifle the wild vibrations from the V-Twin engine. As a result, the motorcycle was noted for its chassis control and stiffness. Its top cornering capabilities were helped in part by its firm Marzocchi front forks and a set of Koni's fully adjustable shocks in the rear.

The Goodman may bear more than a passing resemblance to Velocette's Thruxton due to designer Simon Goodman's grandfather founding Velocette several decades before. Still in limited production for a cost of around $20,000 U.S., the Goodman HDS is a brawny, capable café racer with an unusual pedigree.

1999 WIDELINE TRITON

Decisions over which series of Triumph motor is best suited for specials duty in a Triton is a matter of taste, but this pre-unit custom proves the old mills do have a certain timeless charm about them.

This machine is built around a Featherbed chassis of late 1950s vintage and a Triumph T120 pre-unit engine fitted with Amal carbs sporting open bellmouths. The machine was built only recently but is kept period-perfect by the addition of a set of Norton Roadholder forks clutching a 19-inch Akront alloy front rim. Stopping power comes courtesy of a twin leading shore BSA drum brake, lifted from a BSA Rocket III, which, having been designed in 1968, offered perhaps the pinnacle of pre-disc brake OEM design.

Rather than build a concourse-level café racer, this Triton is clearly ridden hard and regularly, as the owner chose to run a durable, low-cost fiberglass fuel cell from Unity Equipe Company and black fiberglass fenders that can withstand road grime and engine vibration far better than alloy items while looking far less flashy. A bum-stop seat is a standard Unity item known for its stylish looks and less-than-caring feel on the road. The slender headlight mounting brackets, flat-steel mounting plates for the Smith's gauges, and unbaffled central-mounted combination oil tank and battery box are evidence of how far some Triton builders will go in the quest for ever-lighter motorcycles.

6

Legacy

The current resurgence of interest in café racers reveals much about the contemporary motorcycle market. After all, this is the golden age of motorcycling, with worldwide interest in roadracing catapulting MotoGP coverage into a prime-time slot on American television. The domestic market has enjoyed strong sales figures for twelve consecutive years, and there are a plethora of new vehicles that ride faster, look better, and offer superior technology to the motorcycles of any other time in history. Veteran roadracers from Giacamo Agostini to Kenny Roberts have told interviewers that today's modern, high-performance sportbikes offer speed, handling, and braking capabilities far beyond the best, million-dollar race bikes from their heyday, and the future seems prepared to up the lightweight/high horsepower wars with each successive model year.

So why then are a growing number of enthusiasts focusing instead on replicating slower, less advanced machines from a bygone age?

There are as many answers to that question as there are Featherbed specials variations. Perhaps the café racer renaissance is fueled, in part, by the very successes of the sportbike market. It is one of the motorcycle industry's dirtiest little secrets that some of the machines they're offering to an eager public are so fast, few riders possess the skill to enjoy them fully. Speak with sportbike dealers off the record, and some truly startling figures begin to emerge: Some say their liter-class sportbikes have an attrition rate as high as 50 or 60 percent, with the crash rate for the current crop of blisteringly fast 600 supersport machines lagging not far behind.

Exotic and intriguing to look at the French-made Voxan Charade shows what factory café racers would look like if not designed in boardrooms by committees. It's only drawback is not being available in America. Simon Green

I often visit motorcycle salvage yards in my work as a motojournalist, and it is both sad and disheartening to see the large volume of practically new sportbikes, most with only a few hundred miles on their odometers, smashed beyond repair. And because it takes years of track time and careful instruction to even begin to explore the performance parameters of a modern sportbike, many riders are searching for a performance riding experience that's decidedly less taxing on the central nervous system, not to mention their extremities.

There is an inherent temptation to ride a sportbike to its fullest potential, lest the rider feel like a poseur or a fraud. The problem is, as sportbikes grow ever more powerful, this is more difficult to do on public roads. When Kawasaki introduced its evil-looking ZX-10R in 2004, I immediately had to get my hands on one to see what sort of sensations a 170-horsepower streetbike would provide. A habitué of intermediate-level track days and moderately swift road riding, I was, like many motorcyclists, intrigued by the upper-echelon of the performance market. I'd been warned that this 380-pound missile was a truly mind-bending, license-shredding experience, but even years spent aboard everything from Aprilia Milles and Ducati 916s could not have prepared me for the absolutely brutal, violent acceleration this machine could provide. Aim for an apex, twist the throttle, and suddenly find yourself accelerating faster than the human brain could comprehend. Most times, I'd end up a half-dozen feet wide of my intended turn-in point due to the massive thrust beneath me. Wisely, after five months, I became another in a long line of former ZX-10R owners.

A craving for a more controllable level of streetbike performance was a principal motivating factor behind the naked bike movement that surfaced in the mid-1990s. Inspired by the streetfighter movement wherein owners of crash-damaged sportbikes would tear off their asphalt-ravaged fairings and install sets of tall, tubular handlebars for improved comfort and sightlines, the naked bike movement created a genre of motorcycle that borrows heavily on the café racer ethos. After the sales success of the first modern naked bikes like the Suzuki Bandit, Yamaha XJR1200, and Triumph Trident came a desire from the riding public for more evocative styling; Triumph had nailed the retro café racer look—and ride—damned well with the original 900cc Speed Triple of 1994, but few firms were eager to follow.

After three years in production, even Triumph stepped away from the café theme, reinventing the moody, black Speed Triple as the T509, a bug-eyed streetfighter wearing an array of bright, day-glow colors that could give a parrot heartburn. Ducati's stubby, quick-turning Monster did provide a stylish take on the modern café racer theme when introduced in 1993. Riders around the globe fell

The author's all-time favorite factory café racer, the Voxan Black Magic. Clearly meant to evoke the Manx Norton, the 998cc, water-cooled twin can easily be derestricted to produce a throbbing 110 horsepower. Author's collection

The café racer donor bike of the moment, Honda's CB750s are affordable, durable and easy to transform into fire-breathing ton-up machines with just a few simple modifications. Aaron Hollebecke

Fine example of what can be achieved on a budget using a Honda donor bike: second generation café racer clubs throughout the United States are abandoning traditional sportbikes in favor of machines like this Honda custom. Nifty polished rear drum and box-section tail unit add class. Steve Carpenter

Focused on global roadracing efforts and its top-tier superbikes, it took Ducati another decade to realize the existence of a customer base for a more dedicated modern café racer, which arrived with a bang at the 2004 Intermot motorcycle industry show in Munich, Germany. Laid out beneath a dazzling display of halogen lights and posters celebrating the firm's roadracing victories under Mike Hailwood was the Ducati Sport Classics line, a trio of machines that would come to herald the new café racer scene with a bang. The machines, explained Ducati, were designed after carefully studying the custom motorcycles on display at various Ducati Monster Challenge shows and ascertaining the sorts of streetbikes these customers lusted after. Each shared the same wide low Manx-knockoff gas tank, broad leather seat with color-matched seat humps, and a version of the 900 Supersport engine punched out to 1,000cc.

Sporting new, dual-spark plug heads with improved combustion chambers, the Sport Classics were a bold stroke for a company known for looking ahead, not backwards, for inspiration. On the road, the Sport Classics' punchy, 82-horsepower Desmo-valved engine provides the perfect alternative to the manic power characteristics and geared-for-top-speed drive of a full-on superbike. After just a few miles, it's easy to understand why these machines have sold so well.

in love with the revvy little Desmo twin that came standard with tubular handlebars, rear-set foot controls, and an engine that could purr through crowded city streets or maintain pace with sportbikes through the twisties. With tens of thousands of Ducati Monsters roaring out of showrooms each year, a small but dedicated custom and high-performance aftermarket emerged to serve Monster fans, culminating with the Monster Challenge, a series of single-model custom bike shows and a thick catalog of factory-backed parts and accessories under the Ducati Performance banner.

If streetfighters are the true inheritors of the café racer mantle, this cafe'd fighter built from a Suzuki TL 1000S V-twin makes for a hopeful future. Stubby, half-length exhaust canister is won't scrape during full-vert wheelies. Author's collection

One of the Sport Classics, the Paul Smart Replica (named after Ducati's arguably most famous roadracer and adorned in Smart's Imola-winning silver-on-blue livery) became an instant collector's item, selling out the entire 2005 model run in a few months. Ducati's success in the retro café racer market surprised many, but it was not difficult to expect more OEMs to follow in the future.

Harley-Davidson, after all, has built one of the world's largest streetbike empires on a line of motorcycles designed, basically, as retros. Electronic fuel injection and Brembo four-pad-per-caliper brakes may be standard equipment on a number of new Harleys, but to glance at a Fat Bob, Springer Softail, or Sportster model from the current line-up is also to look at motorcycles whose bulbous lines and midcentury style would be recognizable to any bikers from the 1950s.

"Harley-Davidson still builds motorcycles like they did before the war," the late, great Simon

Aluminum bodywork experts like Evan Wilcox are making café racer parts for a growing list of modern streetbikes, heralding in perhaps another generation of customized café racers. Sara Zinelli

"Ronnie" Smith once quipped in the ever-cheeky British *Performance Bikes* magazine. "The War of 1812, that is." Still, there's a steady and growing market for classically styled streetbikes, a fact never lost on the folks from Milwaukee.

The Japanese factories seem somehow convinced that only their domestic Asian market craves true retro-styled machines. Their sole entry into the true retro market was the stunning W650 of 1999. Based on Kawasaki's W1 and W2 Commanders, basically replicas of BSA's Lightning (without the sieve-like crankcases) from three decades hence, the W650 was a brilliant take on the classic British parallel twin. Kawasaki

Expert café specials builders can still create your dream machine for the right price such as this $30,000 Egli-Vincent sporting a Goldie replica silencer and Italian Ceriani forks. Patrick Godet

Though funding for the production version of Kenny Dreer's Norton Commando didn't materialize, the updated 852cc twin is a tempting project for venture capitalists: I doubt we've seen the last of this one. Author's collection

imbued the machine with just the right amount of modern technology: disc front brake, bevel-drive overhead cam, four valves per cylinder. It did this while maintaining a devotion to 1960s aesthetics. The W650 had a functioning kick starter, only one front disc, and the Triumph-replica seat is as uncomfortable as anything from the rocker era. Though riders everywhere had been clamoring for such a machine, the W650 was slow to leave dealerships, particularly in the United States, where it was dropped from Kawasaki's lineup after just two seasons.

It was only two years after the arrival of Kawasaki's retro café racer that Triumph revealed its own take on, well, its own heritage with the reborn Bonneville. Launched in 2001, the Bonneville was something of an unexpected release from Triumph. They had, after all, pretty much covered the T120 look with the popular

Thunderbird line from the mid-1990s. Dismissed by many as too large in proportions with its beefy, water-cooled in-line triple engine and a tall, single-backbone frame it shared with the Speed Triple and Daytona, the Thunderbirds were great motorcycles, especially when it came to the brisk performance of the café racer T-Bird Sport model.

Nevertheless, a certain number of purists had demanded that Triumph develop an air-cooled parallel twin to wear the vaunted Bonneville badge so one was developed.

Though much has been said about the accuracy of scale and devotion to tradition of the new Bonneville, the 865cc machine leaves much to be desired on the performance front. Tested relentlessly in magazines against Ducati's Sport Classics, the Bonneville's somewhat wheezy 59 horsepower is only good for a top speed of 110 miles per hour, not much of an improvement on the final, 750cc T140 Bonnevilles of the early 1980s, which could reach comparable speeds. Triumph has scored a bit better with the Bonneville Thruxton, a café racer take on the limited-production racing Bonneville of the mid-1960s. Upturned exhausts help gasses flow more freely than the standard Bonneville's pipes, and reprofiled cams mean a few extra ponies at the top end. It is clearly styling that separates the Thruxton from its more sedate brother, however, attracting customer money with its clip-on handlebars, racing seat, and full-floating front disc brake.

Both machines, like the W650 before them, roll on spoked alloy rims, which is a brave step backwards for modern motorcycles, but the Kawasaki, it should be noted, trumps the Trumps by offering rims with a slight, upturned lip along the edge, a clever tribute to the beloved Akront rims from the 1960s.

Mecatwin, a small French tuning firm with an eye for timeless café racer cool, has launched a more faithful approximation of what Triumph was attempting to create with its Bonneville. Mecatwin experimented with turning ordinary Harley-Davidson Sportsters into zippy little flat-trackers and the company's take on the Bonneville is no less inspiring. Its Bonneville Racer Special Edition is characterized by its lowboy alloy racing tank, which sits superbly along the Triumph's tall top frame rail. An all-leather racing seat adds to the machine's stealthy profile, while Mecatwin added its own, tastefully machined rear-set footrests, drilled side covers with aftermarket air filters, and braided steel brake lines for added stopping power.

As a small firm, it's a shame Mecatwin has not made its products more easily available; but in the future, it would be great to see the company enter a line of custom Bonneville tuning parts in conjunction with the Triumph factory offerings,

Upon its rebirth by real estate developer John Bloor in 1991, Triumph wasted little time mining its own café racer heritage. This late-model Bonneville Thruxton is powered by an air-cooled, 790cc four-valve twin. Author's collection

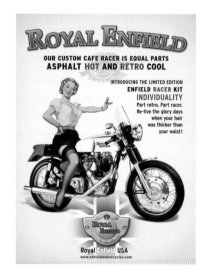

Hip, youthful and full of cool, Royal Enfield has created a niche market for their modest-power 500cc single with ads like this. Royal Enfield Motors Limited

Greg's Customs designed and built this funky, café streetfighter powered by an 1,800cc V-twin from a Yamaha Star Cruiser' trellis frame means serious cornering and light weight. Author's collection

much in the way firms like Ghezzi and Brian have colluded with Moto Guzzi.

The French are far from alone in addressing the café racer potential inherent in these machines. In Germany, builder and parts designer Martin Fischer has launched his own line of accessories aimed at transforming the rather conventional looks of the Bonneville and W650. When viewed up close and in the metal, Fischer seems to have nailed it. With a fetishist's attention to detail, Fischer's megaphone mufflers feature embossed café racer script on each end cap while the aluminum alloy seat units are designed to flow seamlessly into the gas tanks. German engineering means the tanks do not require strapping on with cumbersome and unreliable leather or rubber straps. Instead, Fischer has designed a series of welded-on, threaded lugs that allow the tanks to be bolted directly onto the stock frame mountings.

So beloved is the W650 in Europe that a few of the more well heeled enthusiasts have commissioned bespoke chassis makers to wrap custom steel frames around the bevel-drive twin. Other members of this descendant tribe of ton-up boys had taken their Japanese retros even further in the direction of full-on authenticity, replacing their modern disc brakes with massive, four leading shoe drums from the likes of Grimeca or John Tickle. These sorts of highly effective, low-production stoppers were rare indeed forty years

Futuristic café: A 1,200cc, air-cooled Buell Firestorm motor powers this revolutionary café custom Buell from Ludovic Lazareth. The single downtube front end with rim-mounted six-piston brake caliper offers adjustable steering head angles and is matched with a single-sided rear swingarm that features adjustable length. Motor is supercharged, naturally. Author's collection

Guzzi's VII Sport wowed the audience at its Milan show launch. Close to the target, for sure.

After years of building choppers for high-profile TV program Biker Build-Off Canadian motorcycle artist Roger Goldammer tried his hand at café racers, creating Goldmember, his fast, innovative single-cylinder Bonneville racer. A single front shock mounted beneath the steering head and curved girder forks are among this machine's amazing details. Goldammer

ago, and the costs—not to mention mechanical problems—in mounting one to a modern motorcycle reveals just how strong the café racer legacy is.

It's surprising that motorcycle designer and all-around nice guy Erik Buell of the eponymous American motorcycle manufacturing concern has not mined the style of Harley-Davidson's XLCR Café Racer, though Buell's V-Twin machines are playing quite a different visual and performance game than Harley. The XLCR's unique look has helped that rare machine develop a well-deserved cult status, though any attempt to play upon its heritage is likely to backfire in the States, where the café racer is only today enjoying cult status.

In Italy, however, updating café racers for modern riders has proven effective and profitable

and not just for the aforementioned Ducati. In 1999, Moto Guzzi wowed audiences at the Milan Motorcycle Show with the arrival of the V11 Sport. Basically a standard Moto-Guzzi transverse V-twin sporting familiar trademarks such as fully enclosed shaft drive and the same four-valve lump that's been powering this brand since Mussolini's days, the V11 was a stunner in the looks department. Long, wide, and somewhat heavy in the mold of the original 1994 Triumph Speed Triple, the 1,064cc Guzzi offered a similar level of performance as well;

A natural performance progression of their exciting Sport Café 1100, Moto Guzzi's four-valve, shaft-drive MGS-01 was a bold leap forward for the Italian V-twin manufacturer. Naked street version, please. Author's collection

69 thudding foot-pounds of torque at a lazy 5,200 rpm meant a motorcycle that claws its way to a 130-mile-per-hour terminal speed, which is no small feat for a 550-pound streetbike.

Heft aside, the big Guzzi's extra weight and ample wheelbase made for a motorcycle that swung through bends like a giant magnet was holding it to the road surface and the Brembo brakes proved more than a match for this motorcycle's considerable size. The V11 was a triumph of sorts for Moto Guzzi, and by the 2002 model year that firm had added multi-adjustable Ohlins forks and a matching rear shock to the V11 Cafe, updating the flagship café racer into the V11 Le Mans and V11 Rosa Corsa (Red Racing, roughly translated) models. Not to be outdone when it came to mining the café racer's heritage in the European motorcycle market was Benelli who capitalized on the success of their brilliant Tornado Tre superbike with the Benelli Café Racer.

Benelli was one of Italy's oldest motorcycle manufacturers with a rich racing heritage dating back to the pre-World War II era. When the company wanted to launch a sporty machine that would help the reborn firm attract a wide range of customers, the fairings were ceremoniously stripped from the Tornado and a new set of spiky, deeply angular clothes were fitted along with the name Café Racer. Now to the untrained eye, Benelli's futuristic naked bike bears about as much genetic resemblance to, say, a Royal Enfield Interceptor as an Uzi does a musket; however, in purpose and intent, the Benelli captures the essence of a stripped-down, high-performance streetbike admirably. Graced with the same arm-stretching 1,130cc triple engine from the Tornado Tre (albeit in a milder state of tune favoring midrange rather than top-end rush) the Café Racer buzzes along happily in any gear, with plenty of torque only a whiff of throttle away.

Well balanced and easy to turn in, the Benelli may weigh 430 pounds, but thanks to its high-rear, low-front design and class-leading 24-degree rake, it actually feels like a much lighter motorcycle. The clip-on handlebars are mounted atop the 43-

millimeter Marzocchi forks, mercifully for us older riders, and the steel tube trellis frame manages to transmit direction changes immediately without feeling flighty. Some testers have opined that 1,130cc is far too much displacement for a naked motorcycle, but in its current, friendly, and useable state of tune, its tough to find anything not to like in this machine.

Less powerful on the dyno but far and above the most remarkable of the modern retro café racers is the Black Magic, created by French firm Voxan. Based in Rheims, the Voxan Company is a relatively small-batch manufacturer, churning out less than 10,000 machines each year. All four models are based on the same, 72-degree, water-cooled V-Twin motor, which displaces 996cc with a 98-millimeter bore and 66-millimeter stroke.

The earlier Voxan, named the Café Racer, was an odd-looking bird, with its egg-shaped gas tank and funky, bulbous bodywork. Still, the enthusiast press throughout Europe was impressed by the small company's ability to build a solid, quick motorbike. By 2004, racer Fabrice Miguet had lapped the Isle of Man TT course on a Voxan Café Racer at nearly 110 miles per hour. The next year, I remember spotting Miguet's new Voxan in

Roger Goldammer's Notorious, a rolling, hand-crafted tribute to the Manx Norton. The show-winning custom sold for $155,000, due to its supercharged, 965cc single Harley-style cylinder, hand-pounded aluminum bodywork, and six-speed transmission. Goldammer

the paddock behind the TT Grandstands on the Glen Crutchery Road. I was instantly transfixed by the machine, which is arguably one of the most beautiful café racers, past or present, ever designed. Though the combination of fully modern performance and classic café looks is a difficult one to master—especially considering the emissions technologies, water-cooling apparatus, and other ancillaries necessary to today's motorcycles—Voxan seems to have gotten the formula just right.

The Black Magic's signature element is a mock-alloy gas tank that's mounted high and proud, just like the fuel carriers on a Manx Norton. The tank actually serves as a shroud for the airbox underneath, which feeds a pair of 50-millimeter injectors resting beneath. The overall wheelbase is far from class-leading at 58 inches, but the 420-pound, 106-horsepower Black Magic turns fast thanks to a steep 27-degree rake and a set of 43-millimeter inverted forks from Italy's Paoli and wheels measuring 3.5x17 in front and 5.5x17 in the rear. Though none of this sounds capable of keeping pace with, say, Adrian Archibald's Suzuki GSX-R 1000 or John McGuinness on his Yamaha R1 around the TT Course, Miguet pushed the French café racer to a 114-mile-per-hour lap during the 2005 Isle of Man TT, helping cement the machine's reputation as a serious performer in café clothing.

Voxan has since added to its café range with the full-faired Charade, a handsome retro-classic sportbike bearing at least some of its birthright to the Vincent Black Knight and those dustbin-faired TT racers of old. In time, other manufacturers will most certainly mine this same road for future inspiration, and if this is any indication of the café racer's legacy with the OEM's, we're in for some wonderful motorcycles.

DIY CAFÉ RACERS

Naturally and with a certain amount of accuracy, there are those who will always contend that a true café racer, even in today's technologically advanced age, is a motorcycle that must be hand-built. No thank you, the new breed of café racer builders say to whatever retro-styled flavor of the year comes down the pike. They prefer to get their knuckles skinned, their fingernails dirty, and their pleasure derived from designing and building motorcycles from scratch. Many have met through internet connections. A large number of builders operate small, well-respected shops that build a few café racers each year.

Typical is The Shop, a Milwaukee venture opened by café racer fan Tim Schneider in 1997. Part serious performance center and part neighborhood meeting place, Schneider's shop has tuned engines for Milwaukee's Fuel Café race team and given the café treatment to a number of 1970s Japanese street bikes over the years. Schneider's favorite donor bikes tend to be the air-cooled Honda CB350 and 450 twins, which he says are cheap and available at swap meets and garage sales. Using contacts culled from the AHRMA race scene, Schneider's Shop can wring around 50 horsepower from a CB450 twin by adding big-bore piston kits and flat slide carburetors. They also lessen the machine's overall weight by lopping off the steel fenders and replacing the stock bodywork with fiberglass parts or hand-made replacements. The result is a café racer that bears a striking resemblance to the sleek, silver early Honda roadracers of the late 1950s, an analogy that pleases Schneider immensely.

"The fun of vintage café racers is that their magic is right there where you can see it. They're easy to work on, and when you can make them go fast, it's such a thrill," he said.

Similar thrills have motivated Scotsman Hugh Mackie since relocating to New York's Lower East Side in the 1980s. That's when the British bike mechanic opened Sixth Street Specials, an old-school café racer shop located in what was once one of the Big Apple's worst neighborhoods. At the time, the British motorcycle industry had just imploded and it wasn't difficult to find old Britbikes rusting away in sheds and garages. Mackie, more hoping than suspecting that British bikes would make a comeback, bought as many of the old wrecks and basket cases as he could afford, storing them in a bunker-like sub-basement.

Today, Mackie's name is known among rock stars and actors who wait months to have one of his perfectly restored Triumphs or BSAs, and there's usually a crowd of retro rockers and wealthy motorcycle collectors parked on his front stoop. Mackie's crew has a fondness for flat-track-style motorcycles and raw, rat-rod Triumphs with "all of the gingerbread parts that can get damaged riding in New York taken off and thrown away," though he's constructed a brilliant Slimline Triton recently and has orders for several more. Despite its growing popularity, Sixth Street Specials does not try and gouge its customers or approach vintage café racers as if they were holy relics to be worshipped from afar. Instead, there's a sense of togetherness on display at shops like these where keeping your buddies' motorcycles up and running means more than turning a profit.

The camaraderie that was once such an integral part of the rocker scene seems an inevitable component of the modern café racer movement, thanks, in no small part, to the need to share precious mechanical knowledge and skills. In today's fully warrantied world, there are few youngsters in possession of a working knowledge of the valve clearance guidelines for a 1966 Norton Dominator or the factory oil level for a set of Roadholder forks. Gaining access to

Faux drums on Notorious actually are brushed aluminum shrouds concealing modern, four-piston disc brakes. Goldammer

Harley-Davidson Sportster café racer from Germany proves the venerable American V-twin will continue to inspire specials builders; check out the GSX-R exhaust canister and homemade rearsets. Simon Green

Former AMA 250 champ Roland Sands is a whiz at custom choppers and, apparently, naked bikes like this Ducati Hypermotard that's been treated to a 240mm rear tire on an 8-inch Performance machine wheel, custom titanium exhausts and typically stunning Sands bodywork. Author's collection

that knowledge is integral to keeping café racers on the road. This attitude is typified by British expat Steve "Carpy" Carpenter. A lifetime fan of ton-up culture, Carpenter's father, Dick, had ridden with the rockers during the 1960s. A cross-generational appreciation of fast, stripped-down motorcycles in place, Carpenter became a skilled mechanic and worked for twenty years as a motorcycle courier on the streets of London.

Living briefly in Australia before relocating to central California, Carpenter today holds a firm lock on a lucrative segment of the café racer movement, making his money by purchasing long-neglected CB750 Hondas and transforming them into machines that resemble something from London's North Circular Road, circa 1964. The secret, Carpenter says, is not to attempt building exact replicas of vintage café racers, as the Honda offers a different palate from which to work. Carpenter's machines reveal a workingman's ability to make do with what's at hand. Instead of installing expensive, modern suspension components like upside down forks or monoshock rear-end conversions, Carpy's cafés made do with re-valved stock Honda fork legs that are more than suitable for typical roadwork.

The 750 four SOHC engine is fabled for its response to tuning, and Carpenter has had great success with motors bored out to 836cc, which bumps horsepower levels up to 65 or so at the rear wheel. His Orange, California-based Nostalgia Speed and Cycle has churned out around two dozen CB750 Honda café racers in recent years, and the shop has become a paradise of sorts for seekers of genuine vintage café gear, from Lester mag wheels to Rickman and Dunstall bodywork. There are a few motorcycles powered by British engines in Carpenter's collection, but he's careful to emphasize that the future of the café scene lies elsewhere.

"I could build Tritons and Gold Stars, but that's already been done and the parts are too expensive and hard to find," he says.

Carpenter's having witnessed the rocker era up close as a boy has left him with a great eye for detail, expressed through custom touches like pedestrian-slicer front fender license plates, the liberal use of checkerboard motifs on bodywork, and a penchant for black paint or powdercoat over chrome. Complete machines have sold on internet auction house eBay for less than $6,000, which is not only a steal but somewhere in the neighborhood of half of what I spent constructing

Same as it ever was: The best thing about café racers is getting together with a few friends for a burn-up. Patrick Godet

a true Featherbed-based Triton a decade ago.

Far from typical, or cheap, in the approach to constructing replica café racers is the one followed by Molnar Manx, the British firm behind the Manx Nortons ridden each year at the prestigious Goodwood Festival of Speed. The Molnar clan came to own rights to producing the venerable Manx in a convoluted fashion as café racer chassis designer Colin Seeley first took over the AMC racing concern's inventory and manufacturing rights that were producing the Manx after Norton ceased production in 1966. For a time during the late 1960s, the Manx was manufactured by technician and brake-designer John Tickle, who created the Tickle T5 Manx until he sold the rights off to café racer parts powerhouse Unity Equipe, who carried the single-cylinder torch until Molnar made a successful offer for the brand in 1994.

In the years since, Molnar has ventured into rarefied waters, blueprinting and manufacturing its own version of the 500cc DOHC single. Built according to exact 1961 specifications provided under a unique licensing agreement struck with

What's Old is New Again– The Ton-up Revival

Though the internet is the primary conduit for the café racer legacy to maintain contact, a new crop of publications has emerged, serving readers seldom addressed in mainstream motorcycle magazines. Italy has long enjoyed *Café Racer*, a glossy, photo-filled monthly that offers vibrant photo spreads of contemporary café racers and custom sportbikes. Without a familiarity with the Italian language, the magazine falls a bit short for many readers. Among the more popular titles are *Dice*, published first in the U.K. and now California, and Sydney, Australia's *Greasy Kulture*. Both are hip, small-format, full-color magazines imbued with a Gen-X sense of humor and an enthusiasm for fast, home-brewed streetbikes often missing from large circulation monthlies. Publisher Guy Bolton said *Greasy Kulture* started out as a website back in 2000 but has since become most popular with readers in the United States, Japan, and Europe.

"I've always ridden old bikes—from BSAs to Moto Guzzis, Nortons to Harleys—and have a passion for traditionally styled choppers. I couldn't find what I felt was a quality magazine catering for my tastes, so I produced one myself," he said.

Café racers, like choppers, are big with twenty- and thirtysomething riders these days, a trend Bolton attributes to "discovering their unique character." Bolton continued: "Modern bikes are becoming increasingly homogenized and cookie-cutter in design—and they're discovering the joy of getting these old bikes to go fast. People like Baron's Speed Shop in London, Meatball at Hell on Wheels, and Wes at Four Aces in California are showing the way! The rocker style is ever-popular."

Bolton rides a Harley and a Moto Guzzi café and longs to install a Sportster engine into a Featherbed chassis. Café racers, he's noticed, are becoming fairly common at motorcycle rallies in the U.K. and in the United States, though the Triton has developed its own cult in England due to the generations of tuners still at work.

Bolton sees similarities between café racers and other rat rod customs, despite the differences in intent. "What I love about café racers is that they are the U.K. equivalent of the early bobbers and choppers: Young men stripped down the bikes they had for speed, mimicking the style of the production racers of the day. They're no-nonsense, all business, dangerous, and fast. One of the best bike photos I've ever seen is of a young guy with a pompadour, winklepickers, and a cigarette in his mouth, taking off over a little hump-backed bridge on a Triton. It was taken in the sixties; both wheels are off the ground, and he looks totally at ease. Cool, man."

the Norton factory some four decades ago, the new Molnar Manx nevertheless is rife with modernized technology, including titanium connecting rods, aircraft-grade aluminum for head and cylinder construction, and blueprinted cams.

With their own welding jigs at the ready, Molnar even constructs complete frames using needle roller swingarm and head bearings. Bronze welded from sturdy T45 tube, the Molnar frames are stunning even to traditionalists who own and race original Manx Nortons. Not content to simply play the heritage card, Molnar's racing efforts have long occupied a primary space in its operations, with a pair of the company's machines piloted by Glen English and TT veteran Richard "Milky" Quayle winning the Classic Senior Manx

Grand Prix several years in a row. Naturally, such high-end specifications and attention to detail does not come cheap, and a rolling chassis from the Molnar stable can run as much as $12,000. You supply the engine.

Perhaps the greatest proof that the café racer may finally receive the recognition it deserves can be found in the lucrative custom motorcycle market. Though choppers are still considered the primary focus of the high-end custom motorcycle market, several prominent builders have begun embracing the café racer as an easel from which to create, which is a veritable sea change in an industry often reluctant to embrace new ideas. Former motorcycle road racer and custom bike builder Jesse Rooke made quite a splash for revealing his own take on the café racer with a beautiful one-off machine powered by the water-cooled V-twin from KTM's Super Duke. Rooke has been a regular on *Biker Build-Off*, the popular cable TV showcase for chopper builders. However, instead of simply crafting ill-handling stretch choppers with gaudy levels of chrome and mural paint schemes that resemble something that fell from a customized Chevy van, circa 1974, Rooke, a former roadracer, tends to design custom bikes with a nod toward performance and rideability. That was certainly the case when he revealed his KTM-based café racer.

The tubular, chromoly steel chassis is a Rooke original, designed with a clever single-sided swingarm clutching a WP shock; up front there's a set of 50-millimeter Marzocchi inverted forks with five-spoke alloy wheels by Roland Sands, another *Biker Build-Off* regular with a professional roadracing past who has ventured into the café racer game as of late. Fiberglass was used to construct the squarish fuel tank, which was obviously inspired by the Manx Norton, though the L-shaped seating section is pure streetfighter style as there's no actual seat pad deployed. The wide, 300-millimeter rear tire and shorty, unmuffled dual drag pipes reflect Rooke's chopper background. Wherever this motorcycle is shown, it attracts crowds of enthusiasts from all backgrounds. Though Rooke

was cagey when asked if his machine might someday become a production machine for Austria-based KTM, the motorcycle does sport many of the same components—such as FMF exhausts and radial-mounted Brembo brakes—as their stunning RC8 superbike.

Another high-profile convert to the café racer cause is custom motorcycle wizard Roger Goldammer, who has spent the last decade building high-tech chopper parts and complete motorcycles in Vancouver, British Columbia. A talented off-road rider, Goldammer had longed to infuse some of his competition know-how in the machines he's built for the Discovery Channel's *Biker Build-Off* TV series but feared the reaction to his work.

"At one point, I was doing a show against Matt Hotch, and we were both going to do another pair of fat-tire choppers. I just said the hell with it, I don't care whether people like my motorcycle or not," said the single-minded Canadian.

ExperiMental, the way-out machine that Goldammer revealed on the show, is still being talked about for its two-stroke, Rotax-built single-cylinder motor culled from a shifter kart, and a frame originally home to a Honda CR250 dirt bike. Emboldened by this experience, Goldammer went on to construct two of the most phenomenal custom café bikes in existence. Though both may rankle purists who still view café racers as motorcycles that are British in origin and traditional in design, Goldammer's work will likely influence the next generation of custom café builders and manufacturers who are already taking note of his work.

For a run at the vaunted Speed Week celebration at the Bonneville Salt Flats, Goldammer created Goldmember, a sinewy study in minimalist style, named in honor of movie spy Austin Powers. Goldammer's salt flats racer is equal parts rail dragster and café racer and performs well enough to quash any critics. The machine features more one-off parts than a TT racebike, from its concave-curved girder forks to the hand-welded chassis. For a look straight out of the 1950s,

Fully modern and all café racer is the Wakan, conceived by Joel Domerque in 2005; the 1,640cc 45 degree V-twin features four cams and a dry sump, with the intakes canted at a 43-degree angle; all carbon bodywork, an aluminum perimeter frame and ultra-lightweight running gear makes this a Harley-derivative café racer for the twenty-first century. Author's collection

Goldmember rolls on narrow, 19-inch spoked wheels and runs what appears to be a massive drum brake up front. But inside that machined hub lies a custom, four-piston modern disc caliper. The chassis is a one-off by the owner who designed the duplex cradle with twin shocks at the rear and a removable triangular top section that allows the engine to be accessed easily. Up front, another damper controls bounce for the girder forks but is, like the brake calipers, hidden from view.

Built from narrow-gauge 4130 chromoly steel, the frame is typical of this builder's ability to create very antique-looking components using very modern technologies. The engine is another rarity, based on the crankcases from a Merch Performance Harley-style big bore V-twin, but with the rear cylinder missing. A Rotrex supercharger that's fed pressure by a small intercooler that can also be fed into a nitrous oxide system for additional boost now occupies that gaping hole. Basic power is supplied by a single, 965cc rear jug borrowed from a late-model Harley-Davidson Twin Cam engine, breathing through a single, 54-millimeter intake that's operated by a closed-loop electronic fuel-injection system. The supercharger and single big-bore cylinder are good for a thundering 90 horsepower and 80 foot-pounds of torque without activating the nitrous, and 130 horsepower and almost 100 foot-pounds with the toggle switched on.

Like all good café racers Goldammer runs his machines hard, even though they commonly sell for upward of $130,000. At Bonneville, Goldmember, with its sleek, ribbed aluminum fairings, reached a top speed of 154.843 miles per hour, which any rocker from any age would be impressed by.

Café racers the world over have been most impressed by Notorious, Goldammer's functional, if not highly stylized, tribute to the Manx Norton. This machine is also powered by a single-cylinder version of a Merch V-twin crankcase mated to a Harley-Davidson cylinder displacing 965cc. The cylinder has been rotated back 154 degrees, while the engine's internals include a Goldammer original cam and a bottom end that's been carefully blueprinted and balanced. There's a Rotrex supercharger spinning the engine to an astronomical 12,000 rpm in the vacant rear cylinder hole, producing 83 rear wheel horsepower. A baker six-speed transmission provides slick shifting in conjunction with a Rivera 2-inch open drive belt housed in a custom primary drive made to resemble that of a Norton. The 18-inch Kosman wire wheels feature the same hidden disc brakes as Goldmember and roll on modern, Metzeler radial rubber.

Like the Tritons of old, Notorious features cool, silver alloy bodywork manufactured by hand in Goldammer's studio, where he even

Chopper builder and former roadracer Jesse Rooke revealed his KTM 990 Super Duke based café racer in 2007, stunning crowds with its classic lines and new era technology. Dirt bike exhaust designers FHM built the dual open pipes with Rooke handling the curvy bodywork featuring a convex radiator beneath the café-style tail section. Author's collection

made the two separate oil tanks, one of which is housed inside the 3-gallon gas tank. Instead of housing his complex creation inside an actual Featherbed chassis, a new one was carefully mapped out on the PC, resulting in a chromoly, mock-Featherbed offering 29.5 degrees of rake and holding a set of upside-down WP forks that have been shortened 1 1/2 inches for sharp cornering. You'd be hard pressed to find an exposed brake line, electrical wire, or oil feed tube on this bike, which even runs its throttle cables internally for the cleanest look possible.

This is what modern café retros would look like if they weren't designed by focus groups and corporate boards, as Notorious's high-technology paves a road to the future while the styling keeps an all-important eye on the café racer's illustrious past.

Acknowledgements

This book was a complete pleasure to research as it brought me into contact with some of the most enthusiastic, dedicated motorcyclists I've met in more than a quarter-century of riding and writing about two-wheeled transportation. Their expertise, guidance, and unparalleled attention to detail helped create a historical narrative that would not exist without them. Likewise, many of the photographs included within these pages turned up in my hands through sheer serendipity, provided by café racer enthusiasts from around the world who were simply pleased to hear that a book was being published on their favorite subject. I can only hope that I provided the most accurate, thoughtful, and passionate account of their experiences and, as a result, can help keep the cult of low bars, loud pipes, and fast motorcycles alive for another fifty years.

Special thanks and much props to publisher Tim Parker; photographer Simon Green; Mark and Linda Wilsmore, Ace Café London; Guy Bolton of *Greasy Kulture* magazine; Franck Depoisier at Mecatwin, France; Armand Ensanian and the Brit Iron rebels; Spike, Robert Simpson, Patrick Godet, and Michael Selman at BellaCorse; Chet, Brad, Tony, and Ed; Ian Holcott, Jacqueline Harris, and Hugo Wilson at *Classic Bike* magazine; Burly Burille; Kim Love for her excellent, early copyediting; Nick McCabe and John Canton at Ducati North America; Rocker Bill, Greg Hageman, Dave Degens and Roger Goldammer, Steve Carpenter, Aaron Hollebecke, and Rich Backus at *Motorcycle Classics* magazine; David Hailwood; and Royal Enfield.

Index